In Our Stories Lies Our Strength

AGING, SPIRITUALITY, AND NARRATIVE

William L. Randall

Kindle Direct Publishing
2019

Randall, William L.

In our stories lies our strength:
Aging, spirituality, and narrative

Copyright © 2019 by William L. Randall

All rights reserved. No part of this publication may be reproduced or used in any form or by any means, electronic, mechanical, photocopying, or otherwise, without the prior permission of the author.

ISBN 978-0-973631326

Cover design by CARandall

Contents

Acknowledgments		5
Introduction		7

PART I - Aging, Spirituality, and Narrative

Chapter 1	Aging as a Spiritual Experience	19
Chapter 2	Spirituality as a Narrative Endeavour	35
Chapter 3	Narrative as a Dimension of Aging	48

PART II - Narrative Development in Later Life

Chapter 4	Narrative Development and the Tasks of Later Life	65
Chapter 5	Narrative Resilience and the Challenges of Later Life	82
Chapter 6	The Environments in Which We Story Our Lives	103

PART III - The Practice of Narrative Care

Chapter 7	The Art of Storylistening	119
Chapter 8	The Craft of Storylistening	128
Chapter 9	Taking Narrative Care of Ourselves	143
Postscript:	In Praise of Narrative Openness	157
Appendices		165
References		179
Index		195

Acknowledgements

This book is dedicated to the good people worldwide whose work is to provide older adults what could broadly be called "spiritual care" - work that, in so many ways, revolves around stories. Thanks to Jane Kuepfer of the Research Institute for Aging at the University of Waterloo, and to Kent Mayfield and Sybil Bell of Saint John's-on-the-Lake in Milwaukee, I have had invitations to present at length to such folk on the ideas that are featured in what follows. By this, I mean ministers, rabbis, chaplains, priests, social workers, spiritual directors, parish nurses, counsellors, life coaches, therapists, and others (including doctors and nurses, too) who operate in a wide range of settings, from retirement homes to nursing homes, hospitals to hospice, and congregations to prisons.

I owe a special thanks to Deb Everett and Brent Watts, each of whom has invited me to speak repeatedly, via Skype or in person, to students in the courses they facilitate for Clinical Pastoral Education (CPE) programs in both New Brunswick and Alberta, Canada. This connection led to my delivering a keynote address to the Canadian Association for Spiritual Care at its annual convention in May of 2019 in my hometown of Fredericton, New Brunswick. The response was so encouraging that I determined the time had come to take the ideas that I'd been sharing from the podium - on aging, spirituality, and narrative, especially narrative *care* - and to put them on the page, in hopes that a wider audience would find them useful in the soulful work they do each day. Others who need acknowledging include friends, Charlene Coburn, Colleen Hanna, Gary Kenyon, Khurram Khurshid, Wally MacKinnon, Cindy Lidster, and Karen Skerrett for their comments on one version or another of the manuscript; and my sister, Carol, for designing the cover and taking the photo that adorns it.

Introduction

*It is the nature of old men and women to become
their own confessors, poets, philosophers, apologists, and storytellers.*
-Ronald Blythe (1979, p. 29)

*Life is a book with many chapters.
When one chapter is finished, you must go on to the next.*
- George Vaillaint (2015)

I've been meaning to write a book like this for many years. Now, at nearly 70, the time seems ripe to make it happen: to weave together the three broad strands of thinking that have haunted me for much of my adult life - Aging, Spirituality, and Narrative.

Why Aging? Because, not only am I getting older every day, just like the rest of us, but since 1995 I've made my living teaching gerontology at a small undergraduate university. Why Spirituality? Because, not only was I exposed to religious ideas from an early age by virtue of being a preacher's kid (a "PK"), but after five years of studying theology, I became a minister myself, serving three different pastorates across my native Canada, from 1979 to 1990. And why Narrative? Because, not only does my life trace a particular tale, as does that of everyone else, but it's been the storied complexity of life - what psychologist James Hillman (1975) refers to as "the fictional side of human nature" (p. 128) - that has remained my main focus through all of my scholarly career.

As the three chapters in Part One will consider, these topics are intimately linked, in a circular sort of way. First of all, aging, as I see it, is an intrinsically spiritual experience. Second, the spiritual life has an inescapably narrative dimension. And third, the narrative dynamics of aging - of "biographical aging" (Ruth & Kenyon, 1996) - are every bit as complicated and as critical to consider as the biological or physical dynamics, which are the ones to which I fear we default when envisioning what aging involves.

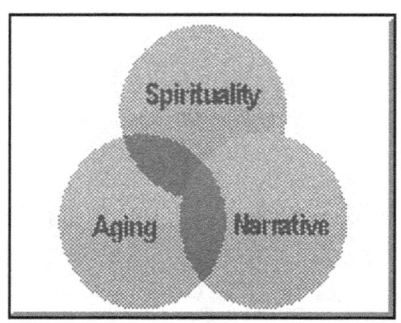

But just as narrative connects aging and spirituality, so too do narrative ideas bridge the gap between the social sciences, plus medical science too, and the world of the humanities: of philosophy, theology, literature, and the arts. As Parts Two and Three will explore in their respective ways, they can also bridge the gap between academia and practice. In Part Two, for example, I will be building on the narrative dynamics of aging that I outline in Chapter 3, and introducing such concepts as narrative resilience, narrative openness, narrative environment, and narrative development; in particular, the developmental tasks and developmental challenges that come with later life - all of which, I'm proposing, are *narrative* in nature. These can serve, then, as conceptual tools or as "theoretical underpinning," as the saying goes, which frontline practitioners can bring to the life-changing work that they carry out in a variety of professions: chaplaincy, counseling, social work, ministry, medicine, and nursing - including parish nursing, too - and spiritual direction. Besides older adults themselves, who are seeking to age as positively as they can, these are the readers at whom this book is aimed. While I trust it will also be of interest to researchers in gerontology, theology, and narrative studies, its principal slant is toward practice, not theory.

That said, I'm not a practitioner myself, and certainly not a clinician. So I can't pretend to understand the ins and outs of what practitioners do on a daily basis with those whom they serve, though from my time as a minister I can certainly appreciate the complexity of their work. The thinking I offer in this book will, I hope, be of value to them nonetheless - especially the thinking about "narrative care," which is the focus of Part Three and which I see as *core* care, since it goes to the heart (the coeur) of who a person is. But I offer all of this thinking in an open-handed manner. If it provides practitioners with a framework and a language to articulate (and, as the case may be, defend) what their work entails - in a healthcare setting, for example - then, so be it. I'll be more than content.

After a keynote address that I delivered not long ago to the Canadian Association for Spiritual Care, an organization primarily for practitioners, a delegate asked me which of the books I had published to date best captured what he'd heard me spouting in my speech. "Actually, none of them does," I admitted, resolving then and there to rectify the situation. Whether he knows it or not, that man's question was the spark that got this book going.

This potential of a narrative perspective - of the narrative *paradigm*, as I think of it - to build bridges across the humanities, the social and medical sciences, and the realm of practice, too, has intrigued me for quite some time. So, then, since every book is rooted in autobiography, let me sketch ever-so briefly the story of my life, or at least the story of my life in *narrative*.

THE STORY OF MY INTEREST IN STORY

My interest in narrative is that one I've come by rather honestly. For starters, I grew up in rural New Brunswick, one of Canada's four Atlantic Provinces, well-known for their down-to-earth, story-rich culture in which entertaining one another through the telling of tales (however "tall") is a talent that's traditionally been prized. But I also grew up as a son of the manse, my father a gifted raconteur who could spin the most innocuous occurrence into a riveting, frequently comical, tale. More than this, as a pastor in a series of rural communities, he actively employed narrative as an instrument of connection, entering parishioners' worlds through the door of story. Indeed, he once told me that saw himself as a "community 'storian" more than <u>his</u>torian. On starting out in a new pastorate, for instance, he would ferret out the storykeepers of the community, most commonly its eldest citizens - its Elders - so that he could ground himself solidly in their knowledge of its past.

But it was more than the genealogies of its founding families or the chronology of its key events that he was keen to understand. Though he recorded all of these faithfully, preparing countless home-made charts to keep track of who begat whom, and though he established the Harvey Historical Society, with these charts supplying core data for the numerous family histories that have since been compiled, it was the anecdotes between the lines that gave him the most pleasure to learn. I mean, those that were richest in local colour, like the time that Jack Lister spied a panther prowling behind the barn, or the night Bert Messer's chicken coop caught fire, or the morning Mary Coburn gave birth to triplets on the kitchen table. For a decade following his retirement in 1985 - "retirement" being a misnomer, of course, for he went on to serve some fifteen more parishes on weekends up until his early 90s - he took pride in writing these stories up and sharing them with others through his weekly column in a publication distributed by a local service club: *The Lion News*. In effect, he became a storykeeper too, and in that regard an Elder.

This passion for story got channeled into chronicling the past of the Randall family itself, plus my mother's family too, in a volume that he published with the assistance of my sister called *Guidelines to Our Ancestors*. When my mother made it known later, however, that she actually had little interest in her own family's past, as per Henry Ford's infamous claim that "history is bunk," he quietly deleted the bits about *her* ancestors and re-titled the book *Guidelines to MY Ancestors* (Randall, 2004). At the urging of my sisters and me, he wrote his autobiography as well, a book bursting with stories, big and little, from his life. He titled it *Showers of Blessing: Memoir of a Preacher, Teacher, and Singer* (2000). "Showers of Blessing" was an old-time gospel tune that served as the theme song for the 15-minute radio program that he and mother aired five days a week for more than 20 years, regaling the surrounding region with pieces of sacred music that listeners would write in and request. In short, Narrative was my father's middle name. Indeed, his longevity (he lived to 98) was due in no small measure, I've since decided, to having *a good strong story* about his life - a concept that I'll come back to frequently throughout this book.

You could say, then, that interest in Story was encoded in my genes. Plus, some of it I fell heir to - sideways, as it were - through my sister, Carol.

A victim of polio at the age of 8, along with my sister Donna and me, thanks to a pandemic that swept through the area before the Salk vaccine was available to stop it, Carol was so paralyzed at the outset that the only parts of her body she could move at all were her neck and one or two fingers on her left hand. But, even if she didn't know it at the time, she fell prey to the narrative bug as well.

Now in her mid-70s and increasingly disabled due to Post-Polio Syndrome, where the original paralysis returns in reverse order to constrict its victim's mobility, she has led an active, vigorous life, rarely bemoaning her fate or trotting out the "victim" card. The archetypal self-made woman, she capitalized on her natural aptitude for statistics and became the first ever female to work for the National Hockey League in anything other than a secretarial capacity. At present, despite physical limitations that multiply by the day, her life is filled with narrative endeavours.

Among these has been a 264-page history of bowling in the province of New Brunswick, plus a 1300-page, 4-volume, house-by-house history of the neighbourhood where she and her saint of a partner, Eldon, lived for nearly 40 years - in Fredericton, the same city where I live too. As I've been writing this book, she's been putting the finishing touches on her autobiography as well, a document teeming with details from every corner of her past. With the title of *Coming Full Circle: Diaries of a Polio Survivor* (in preparation), it will be a good strong story, to be sure. Not only that, but she has been a strong character in my own story as well, seeding it with themes that it might not be seeded with otherwise.  I've sometimes wondered, for instance, whether my decision to enter the ministry was due in some way to assuaging the "survivor guilt" that I've felt all my life for coming through polio essentially unscathed. As for Donna and how she too has been a character in my narrative, seeding it with themes unique to my relationship with her - that, as the saying goes, is a whole other story, one that I'll come back to later.

With avid narrativists like Dad and Carol in my life, it's no wonder, then, that when I attended seminary in my mid-20s, my attention was grabbed by what scattered voices here and there were referring to as "narrative theology," an approach to thinking about spirituality that I'll say more about in Chapter 2. And when I completed my studies and set out on the adventure of parish ministry, this interest in narrative only intensified, not theories about narrative, however, but the real thing. For eleven years, in three different pastorates, with nine separate congregations, and well over 2000 parishioners in total, I listened to more people's stories than I can possibly recall. Listening - sometimes advising, occasionally critiquing, frequently reframing, but always listening - was the heart of what I did. However clumsily I practiced it, and before I had any kind of label to apply to it, I was engaging in *narrative care*.

Eventually, though, I wearied of being on call and on display all hours of the day, of being all things to all people at all times. So I decided to return to university and resume my studies, this time not in theology, though, but in the philosophy of education. It's a whole story in itself, of course, as to how this transition came about, but as it did, the question soon arose: which topic should I research? Through a series of synchronistic encounters that still astound me whenever I recall them and that would take a whole chapter to properly recount, I concluded that *Story* itself was what I wanted to investigate; in particular, the familiar phrase "the story of my life." What is *in* that phrase? I asked myself incessantly. Why do we use it and what do we mean when we do? How are "a life" and "a story" alike, and how are they not? Such questions became an obsession, and the obsession led to a thesis, later a book, that I entitled *The Stories We Are* (Randall, 2014/1995). For we do not just *tell* stories and we do not just *have* stories, I had come to realize, but on some level we *are* stories, too. Our stories and our selves are intimately linked - which is the one sure theme that has run through my thinking ever since.

Cliché as it sounds, writing *The Stories We Are* marked the start of a whole new chapter in my life, if not a whole new story. For it has led me down the labyrinthine paths of nine other books, some 60 articles and chapters, and umpteen presentations to practitioners and academics. And it has brought me into contact with minds and ideas that have stretched my horizons in ways I couldn't possibly have imagined from the trenches of parish life. That chapter got underway in earnest when I came to St. Thomas University in 1995 and began teaching courses in gerontology, among them one called *Narrative* Gerontology, which I have taught on an annual basis for more than a quarter of a century. But I've taught other courses too, such as Aging and Health, Adult Development and Aging, Learning in Later Life, and Counseling Older Adults. So, even if I seldom work with older adults as directly as I did in my ministry days (apart from attending to my own aging parents, that is), my mind remains intrigued by aging in all of its complexity and depth, my own aging included. As I'm fond of telling my students, or anyone else for whom "gerontology" is basically a foreign term, it's one of those subjects that we all become more interested in whether we want to or not.

And this new chapter began, for certain, when I met my colleague, and now dear friend, Gary Kenyon. Gary and I have enjoyed scholarly collaborations that continue to this day and that have played some modest role, I like to think, in drawing people's attention to a more inspiring way of viewing aging than what typically prevails. According to it, aging is seen, not as it usually is, in predominantly physical-medical terms, but in literary-poetic ones, with our lives themselves as flesh-and-blood novels that we're squarely in the middle of, composing them as we go, as author (or co-author), narrator, protagonist, editor, and reader, more or less at once. To borrow from Anton Boisen (1936), founding figure in the field of clinical pastoral education, they are "living human documents."

With Elizabeth McKim, also a dear friend and, at the time that we were writing it, a professor of English at St. Thomas, I was able to take this perspective a few steps further in a book which we entitled *Reading Our Lives: The Poetics of Growing Old* (Randall & McKim, 2008). In it, we spell out more extensively the background to ideas that I'll be working with here, ideas that concern, at bottom, the literary complexity - or the *poetics* - of our lives, especially as we age. To set the stage for these ideas, though, I need to cite some core assumptions that inform my thinking in this book.

CORE ASSUMPTIONS

First of all, stories are ubiquitous. They are everywhere. There are the stories that we share with one another over coffee, the stories we read about in the news, the stories we watch on TV, and the stories we absorb by osmosis from every conceivable side, including those of the spiritual traditions, the political ideologies, and the scientific theories that, in one form or another, swirl around us and inside us. Not only do we live in stories, in other words, but stories live in us. Our lives are steeped in stories, perhaps all the more so as we age, with layer upon layer of them within us - from the one about what happened just last evening to those about history as a whole. Indeed, the lion's share of History, both the subject and the word, is Story. Our existence is storied through and through, and narrative, you could say, is the amniotic fluid of our being.

Second, our lives themselves are inseparable from our *stories* of our lives. The stories that we tell and internalize about our lives, that we remember and imagine, are integral not just to our identities, but also to our actions, our emotions, our relationships, our whole way of being in the world, whether for better or for worse. For "stories are not innocent" (Rosen, 1986,

p. 236). The stories of our lives - our *lifestories,* if you will - can either empower us or imprison us. To adapt a dictum from the philosopher Ludwig Wittgenstein, the limits of our story are the limits of our world. It matters a great deal, therefore, how we tell our stories.

Third, we are always in the middle of our stories and our stories are always changing, whether toward a more open narrative world or a narrower, more restricted one instead. And they are changing on the outside and inside alike. They are changing not just in terms of the events that make them up but of how we make sense of those events as well. For this very reason, simply conceiving of our lives *as stories* can itself have a freeing, even transformative, effect. It affords us needed breathing space between the raw facts of our existence and the interpretations that we weave around them, the stories in which we wrap them up. A bad patch which we're undergoing - with our health, our marriage, or anything - can be viewed later on as but one chapter in our lifestory overall, or even just one page. It is not the *whole* story. And the significance of that chapter or that page - as of our life overall - can be re-storied in a multitude of ways. Where narrative is concerned, nothing is ever set in stone. In early life and later life alike, things can always change.

Lastly, though on a matter of semantics, the terms "story" and "narrative," I suggest, can be interchanged. Some scholars would disagree, of course, seeing narrative as a broader category than story, insisting that not all narratives are necessarily stories. Still, in most dictionaries the first meaning cited under Narrative is typically Story, while the first one under Story is Narrative. Granted, Narrative may sound more academic and thus more important than Story, as in "oh, that's just a story!" But for my purposes here, they come down to the same thing.

As to how awareness of "the narrative variable," as I think of it, has spread across numerous fields beyond gerontology itself, the rest, as they say, is history. So I'll rest my case for now and turn to how aging itself is a spiritual experience.

PART I

Aging, Spirituality, and Narrative

CHAPTER 1
Aging as a Spiritual Experience

Aging can be a growing into the light ...
It is this vision of the light that may grow in our lives
as we are coming of age
and may make a narrowing path into a widening avenue.
- Henri Nouwen & Walter Gaffney (1996, p. 83)

Growing old is one of the ways the soul nudges itself
into attention to the spiritual aspects of life.
- Thomas Moore (1992, p. 216)

Aging is a complex experience on multiple fronts - physical, medical, emotional, and the like. But it is also a spiritual experience. While it clearly entails losses and changes, transitions and troubles, that can bring us to our knees, it has a more positive side as well. Oddly enough, however, this side is woefully underacknowledged by gerontology in general.

Gerontology is an earnest discipline at heart, its attention focused on what we might call the *outside* of aging; in other words, on tangible, practical matters like fall prevention and diabetes management, on policies pertaining to an aging population, and as much as possible, on topics that can be codified, quantified, and fixed. According to no less an authority than Google, gerontology is "the scientific study of old age, the process of aging, and the particular *problems* of old people" (Google; emphasis mine). This fixation on the problematic side of aging, however, always reminds me of the joke about the chap seen fumbling around beneath the street lamp, searching for his keys. When asked where he thinks he might have lost them, he replies: "over there in the bushes." So why are you looking for them here?! comes the question. "Oh," he replies, "because that's where the light is."

Due to this primarily empirical paradigm that dominates the study of aging, we tend to see aging itself in a negative light, its positive potential relegated to the shadows. A "narrative of decline" (Gullette, 2004, p. 28) shapes our story of what aging involves overall, our personal aging included. But that narrative can burrow deep into our psyches and, if we're not careful, cripple us with despair. The side of aging that I have in mind is one where subtler, less measurable, more inner possibilities like insight and wisdom, irony and compassion, begin coming into view. It is the side where we find ourselves assigned an intriguing sort of "philosophic homework" (Schacter-Shalomi & Miller, 1995, p. 124-127) that goes much deeper into the business of aging than mere "brain fitness," for instance. The emphasis placed nowadays on maintaining our mental acuity through doing, say, Sodoku and crosswords and puzzles of various sorts is all well and good. But it is less an end in itself, I would suggest, than a means of equipping us for something else, something more important and profound than, say, "successful aging," "active aging," and the like; something harder to spell out. I describe that something as a matter of - consciously and creatively - *growing* old and not just - passively and resignedly - *getting* old. Our perceptions of aging per se have become so negative, in other words, that we ask far too little of it. As a fully respectable stage of the human life cycle, as potentially its fulfillment, we ought to be asking more.

THE NUDGES OF AGE

Thomas Moore (1992), author of the best-selling book *Care of the Soul*, provides a great jumping-off point for this more positive perspective. "Growing old," he says, "is one of the ways the soul nudges itself into attention to the spiritual aspects of life" (p. 216). I'll leave it to Chapter 2 to say more on what "spiritual" means, and on how spirituality relates to religion. And I'm going to steer clear altogether of what is meant by "soul," Moore himself being a go-to source on the question. Instead, I'll focus here on the many ways in which aging nudges us - not forces us, but nudges us - to attend to sides of it that otherwise get overlooked. Happily, not everyone is overlooking them. Others in the field of aging studies, for instance, have written persuasively on the spiritual dimensions of the aging experience; among them, Susan McFadden, Melvin Kimble, Eugene Bianchi, Albert Jewell, Janet Ramsey, Andy Achenbaum, and Rick Moody, to name just a few. So my aim here is comparatively humble, namely to cite some of the more obvious ways in which aging and spirituality (broadly defined) go hand in hand. And my overriding aim, admittedly, is to set things up so that I can talk about aging as both a spiritual endeavour and a narrative one as well.

More Down to Earth

Aging nudges us, first of all, to become more down to earth. Like many of the ways it nudges us, this parallels what happens to our bodies. With changes to their composition that go by esoteric terms like sarcopenia, osteopenia, and kyphosis, we tend to get shorter as the years wear on, by as much as 4 inches in the case of some. But we can become closer to the ground - more grounded, if you like - in other ways as well, like being grateful for the proverbial "little things" in life: a neighbour dropping off a fresh batch of muffins, a phone call from an old friend, a bird at the feeder, a flower in bloom, a cup of tea, a hug. In the last summer of his life, for example, my father derived great pleasure from the hummingbird feeder that we were allowed to mount outside the window in his room. Each afternoon when I would visit him, he couldn't wait to report what he'd recorded through the day. From a notepad that he kept by his side at all times, he would read off the day's tally: "At 10:27 this morning," he'd say, "one of them took 7 sips. At 1:05, another one came and took 10. Then at 4:14, one took 17!"

As for my mother, whenever I take her to the grocery store, her central agenda nowadays has less to do with purchasing Cheerios on sale or buying a bottle of pickles at two for the price of one, but getting a hug from Cindy or Ida, her two favourite cashiers. As someone who, so I tell people, has morphed into a marvelous bundle of love, she took me by surprise one day after listing off the  various acts of kindness with which people had recently been brightening her world. "Do you know what, dear?" she asked me. No, what, Mom?, I replied. "Well," she said, "I feel like I'm already halfway in heaven." Why's that, I inquired, not a little alarmed. "Because," she said, "I'm surrounded by so many angels!"

More Far-Sighted

But just as aging nudges us to be more down to earth, so it nudges to become more far-sighted. Once more, physical changes provide a parallel. Thanks to conditions with strange names like presbyopia, it becomes easier for us to focus on objects at a distance than those up close - like the words on this page! But there's a philosophical quality that I'm getting at  here. My father, for instance, used to enjoy walking up into the fields across from the manse where we lived, savour some rare time alone, and take what he called "the long view" of things. Psychologist Erik Erikson (1963) has proposed that as we age, it is quite natural, indeed quite necessary, to do this. He called it engaging in "life review," by which he meant stepping back, taking stock, and hopefully concluding that, all things considered, our life has been worthwhile, that it has been what it had to be and that, "by necessity, permitted of no substitutions" (p. 268). Since this process lies at the heart of the developmental tasks of later life, I'll say more about it in Chapter 4.

More Mature Management of Our Emotions

Aging also nudges us to manage our emotions more maturely. Not in all cases, of course, for some older adults can become curmudgeons. But the general trend is to be less blown about by the storms of passion - the mood swings, the tantrums - that can wreak havoc in our lives in childhood or adolescence, and early adulthood as well. To cite the formal gerontological phrase, aging nudges us to have better "emotional regulation" (Carstensen & Mikels, 2005). Along with this levelling off, mood-wise, though, is a greater emotional complexity overall, one manifestation of which may be a tendency toward melancholy. Melancholy, according to Thomas Moore (2017), is a perfectly natural by-product of our soul sifting through the accumulated experience of a life-time, sorting stuff out, trying to make sense (pp. 67-98). Too often, though, melancholy gets mistaken for depression, gets diagnosed accordingly, and gets treated with a pill. Interestingly, the whole emotional complexity of aging is something psychologists of aging have only somewhat recently begun to explore, for it is an enormous topic in itsel, one intricately entangled with the dynamic complexity of our memory as well, something I'll be looking into later in the book (see Magai & McFadden, 1996; Habermas, 2019). And it may well have to do with changes in our intellectual functioning overall, which gerontologists like Gene Cohen (2005) have proposed are linked to changes in the workings of our brains themselves - among them, improved cooperation between our left hemisphere and our right.

More Positive and Selective

Aging nudges us to be more positive too, a trend that is linked to emotional regulation. Gerontologists call it the "positivity effect" (Carstensen & Mikels, 2005), the preference many older adults display for positive feelings over negative ones, and for the positive memories that support or inspire them. Again, not in all cases, since some older adults clearly have a negativity bias, if often for good reason, given the developmental challenges - the *narrative* challenges - with which later life confronts them and which they may receive scant support from others to help them tackle, a possibility I'll come back to in Chapter 5. Still, positivity tends to be the norm. It's the trend to lighten up, to greet life with an air of affectionate detachment, with a gently ironic orientation (Randall, 2013) - in the spirit, if you will, of "there's nothing left to lose." And it's the trend, as well, to divest ourselves of various illusions that we may have clung to hitherto.

Parker Palmer (2018) perceives spirituality in later life as "an endless process of engaging life as it is, stripping away our illusions, about ourselves, our world, and ... moving closer to reality as we do" (p. 54). Death in particular, he remarks, "is the end of all our illusions" (p. 54). Awareness of this alone moves us to start letting go of activities and involvements that bring us down, to declutter our lives of responsibilities and relationships that sap our energies, and to save those energies for things that really matter, that lift us up, not pull us down. The phrase with which gerontologists dignify this otherwise common-sense trend is "social emotional selectivity" (Carstensen, Isaacowitz, & Charles, 1999).

A few years ago, my mother exemplified this theory for me beautifully. Faithful to a fault almost for continuing to keep in contact with people once important in her life, she telephoned an old friend of hers yet again, a friend who in fact never phones her, only to have the woman chide her upon answering with "Why, I haven't heard from *you* in a while!" - as if it were

Mother's responsibility for their not conversing more often. "That's it," she announced to me defiantly soon after; "she could just as easily pick up the phone and call *me*, so I'm not calling her again!!"

More Comfortable With Ambiguity

Along with the emotional complexity of later life is an increasing cognitive complexity as well. Aging nudges us to honour the greyer areas of life, to let go of the need we may have experienced in our younger years for things to be black and white, for people to be good or evil, right or wrong. It nudges us to have more tolerance for paradox and contradiction, in both others and ourselves; more respect for the yin and yang of life; more acceptance of ambiguity and uncertainty (Grams, 2001; Gordon, 2003). It nudges us, too, to see the forest for the trees, to press past the details and to grasp the gist of things, in stories and life alike. Psychologists call this type of thinking "post-formal thought" (Kramer, 1983), and it encompasses the capacity to appreciate metaphor and symbol as well (Labouvie-Vief, 1990). This helps to explain why, of all age groups, older adults are more apt to be drawn to religion, for in religion, symbol is queen and metaphor reigns, and the language employed is nothing if not figurative in nature. Nothing means quite what it seems. In Christianity, for instance, the religion with which I'm most familiar, you can scarcely experience a second of liturgy, recite a sentence of scripture, or sing a stanza of a hymn without encountering expressions that, in any other context, would make no sense whatsoever, expressions like "the wind of the spirit," "the rock of salvation," or "the kingdom of heaven." As we age, however, such sayings may resonate more meaningfully with us as we find ourselves freer to go with the metaphorical flow.

More Inward-Looking

Aging also nudges us to nurture a richer inner life, a richer relationship with our own selves, than we had time to cultivate amid the busy-ness of our earlier years: raising a family, pursuing a career, keeping the wolf from the door. And admittedly, this is not a straightforward nudge to respond to. As former UN Secretary-General, Dag Hammerskjöld, reminds us, "the longest journey is the journey inward" (1964, p. 48) - in many ways, a journey without maps. We can certainly resist this nudge, as many try to do, or as many are conditioned to do by virtue of their profession or their gender or the spirit of the times. It can seem to us more manly, somehow, to rail against aging, to fight it tooth and nail. But the nudging to go deeper, I submit, will still be there, and often grow more insistent.

One day, for instance, I was visiting a retired parishioner whose comical wit and sceptical air I had always enjoyed. Despite being a regular attendee at church, I had never pegged him as particularly religious, quite the contrary in fact. So, when I noticed a Bible lying open on the table beside his favourite chair, I pointed to it and wryly inquired about the seeming incongruency: "Hey, Jim," I asked, "what's going on with this!?" "Well, Bill," he guffawed, "it's 'cause I'm cramming for my finals!"

Something similar has been happening in my own life of late, as I sense my intellectual energies shifting in surprising directions. It's not so much that I'm cramming for my finals but that I'm wrestling afresh with the perennial questions that eventually haunt us all: Why are we here? Where have we come from? Where are we going? It's as if the older I grow, the curiouser I get. On the table beside my own favorite chair is a pile of books that I can't wait to dip into at the end of my day, ones with enticing titles like *Life After Life*, *The Map of Heaven*, *The Other Side*, and *The Cosmic Adventure*. I'm obsessed to a degree that I can't recall ever being before with the bigger picture of it all - not frantically or fearfully but eagerly, excitedly.

It's not that I'm looking for hard and fast answers. On the contrary, for I find the questions invigorating in themselves.

More Interest in The Bigger Picture

Aging nudges us to gaze past the horizon of our individual existence and situate ourselves within a vaster narrative of what *The Hitchhiker's Guide to the Galaxy* comically calls "Life, the Universe, and Everything" (Adams, 1979). Dad's passion for genealogy is a good example. The hunger he had for a fuller understanding of the story of our family became for him a kind of holy quest. The late Lars Tornstam (1996) coined the term "gerotranscendence" to capture the state of mind that Dad was experiencing, one that he proposed develops naturally within us late in life.

It is a state of mind - more a state of heart really, for we may scarcely be cognizant of it at all - in which the boundaries between the past, present, and future are increasingly blurred, our sense of Time itself assuming a different quality than in our younger years (see McFadden & Atchley, 2001). Despite speeding up in general (Draaisma, 2006), time overall becomes less a master or an enemy, less something to be raced against or fought (as in "killing time"), than a friend. We live more "in the center of the moment" (Waxman, 1997), with the future increasingly short, not to mention uncertain, and the contours of the past that much fuzzier to discern, as the events of our lives blend into one another and fade more and more from view. We live more in the now, taking things one day at a time.

So too, says Tornstam, are the boundaries between self and other rendered less sharp. Not in all cases, of course, for some older adults can retreat into a self-centeredness that is embarrassing to observe. But if his hypothesis is valid, then the trend is to experience ourselves, not as isolated and special, but as one humble link in the great chain of being, hopefully having contributed what we could, while we could, to the greater good of our family, our community, our society, our world - a contribution Erikson (1963) refers to by the term "generativity" (see also Kotre, 1984; 1999), a concept I'll come back to in Chapter 4. What is more, the boundaries between life and death themselves may become less sharp, as we sense ourselves inching nearer to the frontier between this existence and whatever one might lie beyond.

More Open to Death

I love what Florida Scott-Maxwell (1968) says on these matters, writing in her 80s in a gem of a volume entitled *The Measure of My Days*. "It has taken me all the time I've had to become myself," writes Scott-Maxwell (at various times in her life a psychologist, an actress, a mother), "yet now that I am old there are times when I feel I am barely here, no room for me at all." She goes on: "I remember that in the last months of my pregnancies the child seemed to claim almost all my body, my strength, my breath, and I held on wondering if my burden was my enemy, uncertain as to whether my life was at all mine. Is life a pregnancy?" she asks. If so, then "that would make death a birth" (p. 76). Elsewhere, she writes about how she and others her age are "people to whom something important is about to happen" (p. 138), how "all is uncharted and uncertain," and how "we seem to lead the way into the unknown" (p. 139).

There's such a spirit of adventure in the things Scott-Maxwell says. It reminds me of what Mr Cain said to me that sultry Saturday afternoon some 30 years ago. After being told by his doctor that there was nothing more to be done for him at the hospital, he had been resting at home, very much on his last legs, with Mrs Cain doing her best to keep him as comfortable as she could. When she called me in a panic, informing me that he had taken a turn for the worst, I dropped whatever I was doing and, as his minister, made immediately for their house. She pulled the door open the second I knocked and ushered me straight into the bedroom. The man lay sprawled atop the covers with an odd sort of grin on his face, as if it were ecstasy as much as agony he was feeling. "I'm ready to go!" he exclaimed, with as much vigor as he could muster. "I'm ready to go!" he repeated - as if sensing that death was less the end of his journey than the gateway to another type of journey altogether.

This same spirit of anticipation, of excitement almost, is expressed in yet another passage from Scott-Maxwell: "A long life makes me feel nearer truth," she writes, "yet it won't go into words, so how can I convey it? I can't, and I want to. I want to tell people approaching and perhaps fearing age that it is a time of discovery. If they say – 'of what?' I can only answer, 'We must each find out for ourselves, otherwise it won't be discovery'" (1968, p. 142). Age as leading us to truth, as a time of discovery?! Not a perspective that gets voiced very often in society at large, with the all-too-present narrative of decline barring us from viewing aging in anything other than a negative light. Yet this is the perspective that needs bringing forward, I believe, and it is one that I'm devoted to promoting here.

More Mature Forms of Faith

Though this could be considered controversial to suggest, aging nudges us to develop more mature forms of faith. I use that word "faith" in the broad sense that James Fowler (1981) employs it in his book, *Stages of Faith*. Following theologians like Paul Tillich and H. Richard Neibuhr, he sees faith as "a mode of knowing" (p. 11) and as "a state of being ultimately concerned" (p. 4); more specifically, as "the search for an overarching, integrating, and grounding trust in a center of value and power sufficiently worthy to give our lives unity and meaning" (p. 5). As such, faith, for Fowler, is a "universal human concern." Put simply,"whether we become nonbelievers, agnostics, or atheists, we are concerned with how to put our lives together with what will make life worth living" (p. 5).

Such a perspective is shared by popular writer, Deepak Chopra (2014), who speaks of faith in equally broad terms as, among other things, "wonder before the mystery of existence"

(p. 252). For Chopra and Fowler alike, we are instinctively faith-ing creatures, whether or not our faithing finds its focus in religion as such. In fact, as I'll be talking about next chapter, religion can often be the problem, more of a barrier to our spiritual development than a boon. By more mature forms of faith, I also mean more mature understandings of the ultimate context of our lives, of the Great Mystery, of The Force, of the Divine, or of whatever we care to call it, if anything at all. In fact, whatever understanding we may have rumbling around in our minds might not have been upgraded since we were very young.

Here, I'm reminded of what New Testament translator, J. B. Phillips (1954), writes in his delightful book, *Your God Is Too Small*, a resource that I found of immense assistance in my ministry days as I puzzled over the range of images of God, many of them quite limiting, that my parishioners tacitly entertained, or had bought into in their childhood and never consciously critiqued. "Many men and women today are living," says Phillips, "often with inner dissatisfaction, without any faith in God at all. This is not because they are particularly wicked or selfish, or as the old-fashioned would say, 'godless,' but because they have not found with their adult minds a God big enough to 'account for' life, big enough to 'fit in with' the new scientific age, big enough to command their highest admiration and respect, and consequently their willing co-operation" (p. 8).

In a similar vein, though from a less likely source, is a perspective voiced by a core character in the novel *Contact*, written by the scientist Carl Sagan (1985). The book was made into a box-office bonanza starring actress Jodie Foster, a movie that I've watched and re-watched I don't know how many times. Foster plays Dr Ellie Arroway, an astronomer heading up a team of scientists involved with the Search for Extraterrestrial Intelligence, otherwise known as SETI. After months of scanning the skies with an array of radio telescopes, the team intercepts a signal of unknown origin that, once decoded, turns out to be directions for constructing a spacecraft unlike anything human technology to date could possibly conceive. Matthew McConaghey plays Palmer Joss, a televangelist assigned to advise the President on spiritual affairs. It's his lot, however, to fall in love with Ellie, whose lot in turn, once the craft is assembled, is to pilot it - which really means to be flung by it through a series of worm holes to the farthest reaches of the galaxy. "Any faith that admires truth," Joss encourages her - after she's confessed to him her difficulty in squaring the doctrines of religion with the discoveries of science - "any faith that strives to know God," he offers, trying to assure her that spirituality and science are not that far apart, "must be brave enough to accommodate the universe. I mean the *real* universe," he stresses. "All those light-years. All those worlds" (p. 420).

    A few years ago, I was puzzled by a cluster of vehicles that were parked each day near some sort of excavation site alongside an isolated stretch of highway a couple of miles as the crow flies from my backyard. One afternoon, unable to contain my curiosity, I stopped by on my drive home from campus to inquire what was going on. A youthful-looking archeologist walked over from the pick-up where he'd been talking with his colleagues and patiently explained to me the situation. Judging from the artifacts that they'd uncovered (scraping tools, arrowheads, ashes), the area had been used as a campsite by antecedents of the present-day Mi'kmaq-Maliseet peoples for fishing and hunting expeditions on the edge of an enormous lake that once covered the valley where our city stands today, in full view, most likely, of glaciers a kilometer in height - some 13,000 years ago. Each evening as I sit on my deck and gaze across the valley, I can't help but think of this tiny nomadic community eking out an existence at the end of the Ice Age so long, long ago. It amazes me, it humbles me. It places the ups and downs of my own little life in perspective straightaway. Yet, set against the age of Earth as a whole, let alone of the universe, 13,000 years is as recent as yesterday - the long view of things, par excellence.

Full Circle and Beyond

Responding to the nudge to envisage our lives within a far broader frame of reference could well lead us to go deeper into our home tradition, whatever that might be. It may lead us to come full circle, as my sister Carol would say; in other words, to return to our roots, and to appreciate, as if for the first time, the rich range of resources - of symbols and metaphors, rituals and creeds, prayers and hymns - which that tradition supplies.

After my father died, I came across a CD of instrumental music among the few new things that he had accumulated in the latter years of his life. He'd probably ordered it through Publishers Clearinghouse, annoying my mother to no end because of the money that he leached from their limited budget to purchase an assortment of items of which they had no real need. For him, though, it meant there would be something to look forward to in the mail every week. The disc featured some of the gentler old hymns that I'd grown up with as a child and that I'd sung in church on numberless occasions - *This is my father's world, Be still my soul, Abide with me*, and others. With expert picking on guitar, and skilful melodies on violin and piano, the pieces are played in a warm, meandering manner, like little works of jazz, their artful riffs improvised around the old familiar air. It's as if they mirror the ins and outs and overall circuitousness of my journey across the years, yet nudge me softly back to certain central verities. For all the wandering and questioning my life has surely entailed, they leave me feeling strangely at peace.

At the same time, aging can nudge us to reach beyond our home tradition and open ourselves to the wisdom within other traditions as well. Once more, my father supplies an example.

When he was in his early 90s, still preaching the occasional sermon in surrounding congregations, I introduced him to my good friend, Khurram. Ever since Khurram and his wife, Naushaba, had moved to New Brunswick from their native Pakistan so that he could pursue a PhD in English, the two of us have enjoyed the most delicious conversations on a broad spread of topics - history, culture, psychology, literature, and religion. We've even published an article together (Randall & Khurshid, 2017). I consider him my spiritual brother. He is also a devout Muslim.

    The first time I took him to meet my father, the two of them bonded at once in the sweetest of ways, the affection they felt for each other palpable between them. The next day, Dad called to tell me how much he'd enjoyed meeting Khurram, and how his curiosity about Khurram's religion had been piqued. "Do you have any books on Islam?" he asked. "Sure do," I replied. "Good, because I'd like to learn more about it." I'm not sure how thoroughly he read what I brought him, and I suspected there was scant chance that he would suddenly convert. But in asking that question and expressing that curiosity he revealed how wonderfully wide his spiritual horizon had become. I felt so proud of him. As someone who had dealt with all manner of people and problems in the course of his career, and who had witnessed the good, the bad, and the ugly within Christianity alone, he was hardly someone to judge another man's religion as a threat. To him, the religion a person adheres to doesn't really matter in the end, for a person is at bottom a person, and the Good Lord loves all of us alike.

AGING AS A NATURAL MONASTERY

    Gerontologist Rick Moody (1995) has described aging as a "natural monastery" (p. 96), a place and time in life, if you like, for stepping back and taking stock. It is a time for "crawling up inside myself," as an elderly parishioner once expressed it to me when I was visiting her at home one quiet afternoon. It is a time for "disengagement," to use a term that gerontologists shy away from nowadays; a time, that is, to enter a more detached, more contemplative space. It is a time to dip into the philosophic homework that has been gathering quietly inside us; to start pondering the several questions - the *slow* questions - that 70 to 80 years of living have planted in our hearts. It is for such reasons, then, that I see aging as an intrinsically spiritual experience.

Not that the physical realities are of no consequence: the aching joints, the flagging energies, the failing hearing and vision, the spotty memory, the loss of cherished relationships and routines. Far from it. But in light of the narrative of decline, it can be tempting to equate such matters with what aging itself comes down to. In light of a narrative of development, however, we can begin to see them as part of the adventure, or at least as part of the "trouble" that is essential for *any* story - in this case, a *life* story - to be deemed a story at all (Bruner, 1999, p. 8). Put simply, no trouble, no tale. Viewed from a broader perspective, in other words, they are not punishments doled out by fickle fate in a harsh, unfeeling universe, but invitations to go deeper, portals to a quality of being Scott-Maxwell (1968) speaks of inspiringly as "fierce with reality" (p. 40).

I've been thinking for some time that gerontologists ought to have more frequent dialogue with theologians and scholars of religion, and vice versa of course, for there is an intimate connection between their respective concerns. We know for a fact, by way of example, that older people who have regular involvement in spiritual practices or religious activities tend to live longer, healthier lives (see Koenig, 1995). They report less stress, less anxiety, less depression. It's as if they feel more at home in the world overall. And they have more extensive social networks and more resources in general, both outer and inner, for coping with the challenges of later life. More than this, there is a connection between these two broad fields of inquiry because aging itself is a naturally de-centering, transcending experience. It is, as I say, an implicitly *spiritual* experience. But spirituality, in turn, has a narrative dimension, which is what I want to look at now.

CHAPTER 2

Spirituality as a Narrative Endeavour

*Telling our stories is an act of transcending the personal
and entering the realm of the sacred.*
- Robert Atkinson (1995, p. 11)

*Each one of us is forced to do deliberately for oneself
what in previous ages was done by family, custom, church, and state,
namely, form the myths in terms of which
we can make some sense of experience.*
- Rollo May (1991, p. 29)

Spirituality is, admittedly, difficult to define. What most thinkers agree on, though, is that it's broader than religion. During my days in ministry, I learned to my dismay, for example, that not all religious people are necessarily very spiritual; conversely, lots of folks whom I'd call spiritual are not necessarily very religious - just the opposite in fact. True, spiritual people often express themselves in religious ways, or draw sustenance from their involvement in religious activities and communities. And, true, there is typically a symbiotic relationship between them. But in the end, the two are not the same.

SPIRITUALITY AND STORY

Given the perspective that I'm putting forward in this book, I side with those who define spirituality in the broadest possible terms, as having to do with our innate need to make sense of things. Human beings are *hermeneutical* beings, in other words. They are interpretive beings, meaning-making beings. But since narrative, as I'll be showing, is one of our main means of making meaning, of wresting coherence from chaos, then spirituality is by extension a narrative endeavour (Lasair, 2019). One writer insists, for instance, that "the very act of story telling is by definition holy;" that it is a "redemptive undertaking" (Carroll). In the words of autobiography scholar, Alfred Kazin, it is "an effort to find salvation" (1981, p. 35). For Karen Scheib (2016), an academic friend and a professor of pastoral theology at Emory University, "to enter another's life story is to enter a holy space" (p. x).

To approach the notion of spirituality as a narrative endeavour from another angle, we tend to take in a spiritual tradition less through the study of abstract doctrines and creeds than through its rituals, symbols, metaphors ... and *stories*. An acquaintance recounts to us her tale of coming to belief, and we may be moved to accompany her to her place of worship and open ourselves to experiencing a similar transformation ourselves. But it's her story that moves us as much as her beliefs. By the same token, the homily or hymn that inspires us does so, not because it appeals to our logic, but ultimately because it speaks to our heart. It does so because it triggers our memories of the past, touches on our troubles in the present, and feeds our fantasies or fears for the future; because it relates to our unique lifestory. We hear the homily, we hear the hymn, not in spite of that story, in some airy realm removed from real life, but within it. We experience spirituality through our stories, not despite them.

For their part, spiritual traditions provide us with not just doctrines and creeds, rituals and rules, but (by means of these) "sacred masterplots" by which we can live, and live within (Brooks, 1985, p. 6). They provide an over-arching storyline of Life, the Universe, and Everything within which to situate our individual story. For those brought up in a particular religion, these meta-narratives or *master* narratives, as some would call them, are often absorbed by osmosis early in life, woven into our "narrative unconscious" (Freeman, 2002), whether for better or for worse.

For over 50 years, my father was a minister with the United Church of Canada, a comparatively progressive Protestant denomination. Theologically, however, he remained in many ways the conservative Baptist that he'd been growing up. For me, growing up with him as the head of the house, his decidedly literal reading of scripture, especially of passages that prophesied The End of The World, wormed their way into my thinking early on, and not always in a helpful manner. As an undergraduate at Harvard, I fell in with the Harvard Radcliffe Christian Fellowship, a variation on the conservative-evangelical organization, InterVarsity Christian Fellowship, which boasted chapters on countless campuses at the time. Partly because of the friendships I formed with fellowship members, I went so far into a fundamentalist frame of mind - obsessed with Satan and Sin, with having the answers to all the big questions, and with proclaiming to others their need to accept Jesus as their Saviour more or less immediately or else be prepared go to hell - that it took years for me to shake myself free (see Barr, 1984).

Since those days, nudged naturally by aging itself, I've arrived at a more broad-minded perspective on things, at a story of myself and my world that breathes fresher air. My concept of The Mysterium Tremendum, for example, is that much more mysterious than in days gone by, and at the same time more immediate too. And my notion of Truth is more open to truths that are treasured by other traditions, not to mention by those who identify themselves as agnostics or atheists, who for their part, however unwittingly, I would say, subscribe to what is still a master narrative; in other words, one that claims there is no God at all, or at least not as conventionally conceived. I'm more open, too, to the knowledge afforded us by Science concerning the nature of the universe, the *real* universe, our common home; more open to the possibility of intelligent life on other planets and in other galaxies, more open to the Multiverse, to a world that is truly "without end."

Narrow or wide, rigid or fluid, the grand narratives of the world's religions are structures for morality, for meaning, for coherence, for making sense of our lives. They offer more or less ready-made answers to life's perennial questions: Who are we? Where have we come from? Why are we here? They offer "narrative resources" (Freeman, 2000, p. 81) and "narrative templates" (Abbott, 2002, p. 7) that we can adopt or adapt for interpreting and articulating what's important in our lives. More or less explicitly, they lay out over-arching accounts of Life, of History as a whole, and of Humanity, with all its potentials and ills. And they constitute narrative environments that we can live within - once more, for better or for worse. They can be either "astonishing resources" or, as I discovered with the fundamentalism that dominated my late teens and early 20s, "rigid, imprisoning structures" (Beardslee, 1990, p. 173). And they can, of course, have conflicting storylines, competing narratives, running through them - the great doctrinal squabbles that I learned of when studying church history, or the vicious civil wars that have ripped entire societies apart, bloodying the pages of the past, as embarrassing cases in point.

While such rifts may be seen by insiders as the sign of an evolving vitality, of a living faith, many of us in our so-called post-modern age can be repulsed by them, thrown into a disillusionment that drives us away from faith of any kind. Alternatively, they can give us permission to detach ourselves from unquestioning adherence to our home tradition, whatever that may be, and move toward a more ironic orientation instead (Prickett, 2002), whereby we draw not just from its own astonishing resources but, eclectically and syncretically, from those of other traditions too, piecing together a framework of beliefs - a larger story - that works uniquely for us.

Just as a given tradition will have competing narratives swirling around within it (and so far I've been using Christianity as my central example, since that's the one I'm most familiar with), so other master narratives will be swirling around within us, including the narrative we call Science. Thinking of science itself in narrative terms, however, may offend those who see it as the anti-thesis of narrative, grounded not in supposition or superstition, in legend or story, but in the cold, hard Truth. Yet no less a scientific mind than Ervin Lazlo (2007) speaks frankly of how theories in science are effectively "fables" - whether "confirmed" or "failed" (p. 17). Along similar lines, science writer, Joseph Schwartz, describes science as "an accumulation of written narratives about our relationship to nature" (cited in Pickover, 2015, p. 21).

Still another science writer, Lynne McTaggart (2002), observes in her fascinating book, *The Field,* that "although we perceive science as an ultimate truth, [it] is finally just a story, told in installments" (p. xix). There's the version of the cosmic narrative sketched out by Galileo, for instance, which Newton's version superceded, only for Einstein's, Heisenberg's, and Hawking's ever more encompassing versions to overtake in turn. Along these lines, thinkers such as Brian Swimme and Thomas Berry, as well as Fritjof Capra, Gary Zukav and several others, have been drawing our attention to how science and religion actually have much more in common than we've otherwise assumed. Swimme and Berry (1992), in particular, call for a narrative that weaves the evolving visions of science with insights into the nature of things that come from spiritual and mystical traditions of various types - "the universe story," as it were. I'll come back to this point later.

NARRATIVE THEOLOGY

To bring spirituality and narrative together in another way, I'd like to take a brief detour here and mention a few of the core insights of what has been referred to as narrative theology, an approach to understanding religious issues that I was exposed to in seminary some 40 years ago and instantly found intriguing (see Hauerwas & Jones, 1989; Goldberg, 1991; Stroup, 1981). If I may, though, I'll start with a story.

When I was growing up in rural New Brunswick, my father, who was also my minister (talk about a dual relationship!), drew upon his love of genealogy to come up with an ingenious game for us kids to play in the youth groups that he organized. After a brief devotional service, which we (not he) would lead and for which we would receive points (so much for a prayer, so much for a reading, etc.), we would divide up into two teams and sit on benches on either side of the church basement. Dad would then call out a question and whichever member of each team whose turn it was to answer would race one another to a table at the front of the room. On it sat the kind of bell that a teacher would use, the kind you ring for service in a store. The goal was for us to have fun, to be sure, so that we would grow up feeling that church was not boring but cool. But it was also to motivate us to acquaint ourselves with the Bible, or at least the Old Testament, or at least those sections of the Old Testament that featured "the begats" - *Abraham begat Isaac, Isaac begat Jacob, Jacob begat Joseph*, and so forth.

"For 5 points," he would announce with the authority of a game show host, the room hushed in anticipation, "who was the father of Isaac?" The two contestants whose turn it was to compete would make a mad dash for the bell on the table, slipping and sliding on the cement floor as they went, one with the word Abraham spinning around in her head, the other with Moses in his. If Abraham rang the bell first, then Dad would shout "Correct!" and cheers would soar to the ceiling from her team. If Moses was first, the answer came back "Wrong!" and groans of disappointment could be heard from the opposing side as the contestant slunk back to the bench.

As a strategy for grounding us in the verities of the faith, it was somewhat superficial, to be sure, for the riches of the rest of scripture - the wisdom of Solomon, the poetry of the Psalms, the Beatitudes of Jesus - hardly lent themselves so easily to this kind of competition. Nonetheless, in its fashion, it made us aware of a central feature of the Bible, which in turn is a central plank of narrative theology. In other words, whatever else it is, the Bible - described by literary scholar, Northrup Frye (1980), as "this huge, sprawling, tactless book" that "sit[s] there inevitably in the middle of our cultural heritage" (p. xviii) - is nothing if not a complex narrative quilt. It is a loosely-woven patchwork of chronicle, parable, prophecy, and myth. And holding it together, as the thread of the plot (more or less) is a single, over-arching storyline, meandering in nature but all-encompassing in scope, that traces the saga of humanity, or at least of "God's people," from Beginning to End: from the creation of the world, as outlined in Genesis, to Armageddon and the Second Coming of Christ, as envisioned in the book of Revelation.

Of course, it's infinitely more complicated than this, as Biblical scholars of every stripe are certain to attest. For woven through it, layered into it, are different macro-stories within the Old and New Testaments alike, different overarching versions of God, of the mission of Jesus, of the history of the early Church, and so on and so forth, each with its unique vision and bias. Nor can the historical context reflected in the various books of the Bible be disentangled from the cultural-political-historical context of the Mediterranean region as a whole.

On that note, but going beyond the Bible itself, a narrative theology acknowledges that there are also multiple versions of Christianity in general, of its message and meaning, discernibly at work as we move from one corner of Christendom to another. Orthodox Christians operate, you could argue, with a different overall version of the Christian story and the Christian life than Roman Catholics do, who for their part operate by and large with different versions than Protestants do. And clearly within Roman Catholicism and Protestantism alike, both historically and at present, any number of sub-versions and sub-sub-versions can develop, with the history of sects and splits of various sorts serving as solemn reminder.

On any given Sunday, the "good news" will get refracted through the larger stories of the particular tradition in question (Roman Catholic vs Protestant), the particular denomination (Presbyterian vs Baptist), and the particular congregation (St. Marks by the Lake vs St. Andrews on the Hill) (Hopewell, 1987). In turn, it will be filtered through the life story of the particular preacher in the pulpit and of each parishioner in the pew - who more than likely will get more out of the stories with which the sermon is, hopefully, laced than from the dogmas that these stories supposedly flesh out. For each of them, moreover, God will be experienced in different ways, depending on a host of inscrutable dynamics that relate to his or her distinctive storyworld. One aspect of this experience, for instance, could be the sense, more or less intense, that God is not just an abstract concept to be contemplated from afar but a living presence in one's life, a core character in, if not co-author of, one's own life story; conversely, that one is a character, however minor, in God's story too.

Along similar lines, to "convert" to Christianity - and let me reiterate that I'm citing Christianity merely as an example, for the same process is presumably true in other traditions too - is to re-interpret, to revise, our personal story in light of the larger story that lies at Christianity's heart. Or at least the peculiar version of it that's touted by the denomination with which we happen to be associated. Henceforth, as happens often in Fundamentalist circles, we may view our lives as having a clear Before and After. A sharp shift in our worldview takes place: *I once was lost but now am found, was blind but now I see.* My story is no longer just my story but God's story as well. In a sense, my story and God's story come together. A convergence of versions - a con-version - occurs.

That said, spirituality is no once-and-for-all affair. It has a dynamic dimension. So, in terms of the point that I've just been making, to "grow in faith" can involve a regular re-working of that con-version relationship, as our understanding of both our My Story and The Story evolves. Thus, as our knowledge expands with time of countless things - of human nature, of our own nature, of Nature period - a continual re-storying will be at play in the direction, ideally, of ever vaster, more encompassing versions of our lives and our world, and of Divine involvement in both. One thinker whose insights I greatly admire in this regard is John Haught.

I recall reading Haught's book *The Cosmic Adventure* as a minister back in the 80s and being excited at the wide open vision of the bigger picture that he sketched out in it (1984). That vision breathed fresh air into the tidy, parochial view of the world that my parishioners seemed quite comfortable with, or at least unwilling to critique, and that I too felt constrained by in preparing my homilies week after week. At the time (I hadn't yet read McTaggart's work), I was drawn to books like *The Dancing Wu Li Masters* by Gary Zukav, or *The Tao of Physics* by Fritjof Capra, or *God and the New Physics* by Paul Davies. These works were, quite literally, blowing my mind about the mysteries of the physical universe, from the helter-skelter quality of the sub-atomic realm to the graceful spinning of entire galaxies, themselves numbering in the billions, with the untold worlds and unnamed beings to which they, in turn, were home. All of it, continuing to expand and complexify from a beginning (a Big Bang?) that is next to impossible to conceive to an end (a Big Crunch or Big Freeze?) that is no less difficult to envision. But the parameters of the spiritual tradition I had inherited and was obliged to expand upon, if not defend, by virtue of my position, were far too restrictive to command my unquestioning allegiance. They did not easily allow one to accommodate the exhilarating picture that scientists were painting of the nature of things. I needed a bigger story overall, one in which the insights of science and religion alike could find a common home.

Haught's book helped me to address that need, as has his most recent book as well: *The New Cosmic Story: Inside Our Awakening Universe* (2017). In it, he describes "nature as a gradually unfolding narrative," as "narrative to the core" (p. 71), and the universe as "an unfinished story whose meaning is far from having been set in stone from the start" (p. 7). This unfinished universe story, however, has an outside and inside dimension, as does aging itself. Scientific theories and knowledge focus on the outside, on the "how" questions, as it were; while religious traditions, each in their fashion, focus on the inside, on the "why." What we need, says Haught, and what may well be emerging before us is "a narrative that tells the whole cosmic story, inside as well as outside" (p. 2). With an understanding of narrative that is eminently compatible with the one that runs through this book too, Haught has this to say: "As we follow a story (for example, in a book), its meaning at any present moment may be dawning, but it still lies mostly out of range. Reading the cosmic story," he says, "calls for a similar kind of waiting, a policy of vigilance inseparable from what some religious traditions call faith" (p. 39).

As we can see, then, the permutations and combinations - and the possibilities - in something as seemingly simple as "faith" are bewildering to entertain. For in viewing spiritual matters through a narrative lens, we open a Pandora's Box of questions to consider. One question that I'd like to introduce quickly before proceeding concerns our own life stories as parabolic.

LIVES AS PARABLES

One of Jesus' central pedagogical tools was the parable, the tale of the Prodigal Son or the Good Samaritan as ready examples. But what is a parable? A whole set of scholarly inquiries have emerged on this one question alone. Yet two or three insights can be singled out as launch pads for my thoughts next chapter on the narrative complexity of growing old. One scholar refers to parable per se as "a fundamental instrument of the mind," of the *literary* mind, that is (Turner, 1996, p. 5). But this understanding of parable takes us down a rabbit hole that, once more, we have neither time nor space to investigate here. On a commonsense level, however, a parable per se, if not parable in general, is an extended metaphor, a metaphor in story form. Like metaphors in poetry or metaphors in sacred writings, or even metaphors in science, a parable takes us from the realm of the known to that of the unknown. It pulls us into a world that seems familiar enough on the surface - a father and two sons, for example, or a man who's been robbed and left for dead on the side of the road. But it spews us out the other side with, very often, a transformed understanding of the order of things. It's not the older brother who has stayed home, worked hard, and kept his nose clean for whom the father throws a feast, but the younger, wastrel one instead. And the person who helps the man who's been robbed is not the Pharisee or the priest, which is who the story's original listeners would have expected, but the one deemed to be "unclean" - the Samaritan.

Whether we're thinking about the parables of Jesus or those of the Sufis or of any other tradition, if such stories work in the way that the storyteller intends, then they shake the foundations of our values and call into question our assumptions about the way the world works (see Crossan, 1975). At the very least, with their distinctive combination of "formal closure" and "philosophical openness," they set our minds thinking (Morson, 1994, p. 228). They cause us to inquire within. And there is no end of questions that they nudge us to consider, of possibilities to entertain, meanings to glean, things to learn. In this way, as one scholar puts it, the parable interprets us, not the other way around (TeSelle, 1975a, p. 71).

Clearly, though, it's not just stories from sacred traditions that possess this sort of parabolic potential but so can secular stories as well. Sitting in my beloved coffee shop working on this book, I noticed an older gentleman sitting at the table across from me one day, reading Paul Coelho's (1997) little book, *The Alchemist* - a book that I have on my shelf at home but haven't yet read. Knowing a little bit about the chap from previous exchanges, I expressed curiosity about his choice of text. Good book?, I asked. "Oh yes," he replied, a wide smile on his face; "this is my third time reading it!" "Why's that?" I replied. "I don't really know," he said; "it just somehow *speaks* to me." The book, I would say, was a serving as a parable for him, its narrative world assisting him in ways that I'll never understand to make sense of things in his own world too, raising questions, sparking insights, giving voice to issues and themes that may have been swirling around inside of him for years.

Any novel or any movie, like *Contact* for me, can do the same for any of us at any time - a biography, an autobiography, a fable or fairy tale, you never know. For some, it may be *The Lord of the Rings* while, for others, *Star Wars* or even *Harry Potter*, that offers them a storyworld sufficiently expansive to situate themselves inside of it, to seed their imagination with a sense of Right and Wrong, Good and Evil; to inspire them, through its characters and the plots in which they are enmeshed, to be all that they can be, with integrity and courage (see Johnston, 2014). The parabolic potential of all stories, therefore, cannot be stressed enough, including our own stories too (Randall, 2014; TeSelle, 1975a, pp. 145-181).

In introducing the idea of our own life stories as parabolic, as sacred texts (Atkinson, 1995, pp. 29-40), I'm suggesting that the narratives in terms of which we understand our identity are, like parables, amenable to multiple readings. The more deeply we delve into the stories of our lives - remembering them, reviewing them - the more questions we stand to uncover, the more discoveries we are likely to make, and the more open we are bound to become - more *narratively* open, as I'll be considering soon. This is in keeping with Mark Freeman's (1994) delicious suggestion that "our lives [are] like richly ambiguous texts to be interpreted and understood, whose meanings are inexhaustible," and "whose readings cannot ever yield a final closure" (p. 184).

An 80-something woman participating in a workshop entitled "Restorying Our Lives" that Gary and I were leading several years ago announced to the rest of the group over lunch that she had recently completed her autobiography. Immediately, the room erupted in hearty applause. As soon as it subsided, she made a follow-up announcement. "And now," she said, "I'm ready to start it all over again!" Here is how memoirist Patricia Hampl (1999) articulates the situation in her book, *I Could Tell You Stories: Sojourns in the Land of Memory*: "If we learn not only to tell our stories," she writes, "but to listen to what our stories tell us - to write the first draft and then return for the second draft - we are doing the work of memory" (p. 33). My point is that the work of memory is never done, for there is no end whatever to what we can learn, not just about ourselves, but in a sense *through* ourselves; no end to "autobiographical learning" (Randall, 2010a). In responding to the nudgings of age, in other words, there is no end to how much we can *grow* old and not merely *get* old.

Not long ago, I was presenting on these themes to practitioners who provide spiritual care to older adults in a variety of settings. During the break, a delegate shared with me a quote from theologian, Frederick Beuchner, that she felt summed up the perspective I'd been attempting to get across. I can think of no better way to end this chapter and nod toward the next than by citing it here: "Let us read with open minds," Beuchner says, "the book our life is writing ... and learn."

CHAPTER 3

Narrative as a Dimension of Growing Old

Every life has a story.
- A & E Biography

It matters how we tell the story.
- Janet Ruffing (2011, p. 93)

Aging is a multidimensional experience, for we age and change on several fronts at once - physically, cognitively, emotionally, socially, and, as I've just tried to show, spiritually too. Another way we age, however, is autobiographically. In other words, we age and change in terms of the stories by which we understand our lives: past, present, and future. Though this type of aging, sometimes called "biographical aging" (Ruth & Kenyon, 1996), has only somewhat recently begun to be looked into, it is every bit as intricate as biological or physical aging, if not far more so in fact, though it is of a different order, like apples and oranges, and thus difficult to compare. And as Chapter 1 hinted, it is linked to spiritual aging too (Staude, 2005) - the *Confessions* of St. Augustine as a classic case in point. It is certainly as critical to incorporate into our equations in studying what aging involves overall. The branch of gerontology devoted to considering biographical aging is narrative gerontology (see Kenyon, Bohlmeijer, & Randall, 2011).

NARRATIVE GERONTOLOGY

As someone who has played a modest part in advancing this approach, I think of it as offering a whole different starting–point for understanding later life. And it opens up a conceptual space for talking about topics that are more at home in the humanities than in the social sciences. The topics I have in mind tend to fall outside the empirical-statistical paradigm that dominates gerontology in general, which, as I mentioned, perceives aging as, implicitly, a "problem to be solved" (Cole, 1992, p. 241) - medically, financially, politically, etc. For instance, besides enabling us to talk about spirituality - given that spirituality has to do with meaning and that narrative is a key means of making it - a narrative perspective enables us to talk about wisdom as well.

In an insightful book titled *Beyond Nostalgia*, Ruth Ray (2000) describes a study that she conducted into the process of self-exploration experienced by women who were engaged in a life-writing group of which she herself was a member. A literature scholar-turned-gerontologist, Ray witnessed first hand how writing about one's life, reading aloud what one has written, and then comparing notes with others in a respectful, supportive environment - what Gary Kenyon and I would call a "wisdom environment" (Randall & Kenyon, 2002) - invites a novel understanding of what wisdom is. For Ray, wisdom is related to a kind of narrative fluidity or narrative openness - a quality I'll be looking at more closely in Chapter 5. It is related to the capacity to entertain what anthropologist Mary Catherine Bateson (2007, p. 213) calls "multiple fluid narratives" about one's life. "A person is truly 'wise'," writes Ray, "when she is able to see life as an evolving story and to create some distance between self and story by reflecting on it from multiple perspectives" (2000, p. 29). 'Wise' people," she goes on, "watch themselves tell life stories, learn from others' stories, and intervene in their own narrative processes to allow for change by admitting new stories and interpretations into their repertoire" (p. 29).

Envisioning wisdom as having to do with the kinds of stories that we have about our lives, or more accurately, with the relationship that we have with our lives *through* our stories, is one example of the many intriguing possibilities that come to mind once we take seriously the narrative complexity of later life. But perhaps a bit of background from the field of narrative psychology would set the stage for thinking about them.

NARRATIVE AND EVERYDAY LIFE

Like both narrative gerontology and narrative theology, narrative psychology sees human beings as *hermeneutical* beings. They are - we are - makers of meaning, certainly in ways that the sparrows at my feeder are not, let alone the squirrels who chase them away! Or at least they're not makers of meaning in a manner I can easily grasp. It's entirely possible that squirrels possess an ability to wield language that parallels my own, that they can formulate stories about their lives and share them with their chums; that, in their own fashion, they are just as narratively complex as me. But I'll leave it to the experts in squirrel psychology to say for sure if this is so. In the meantime, it seems that we do indeed stand out from our fellow creatures. We are "the story species" (Gold, 2002), equipped with "the literary mind" (Turner, 1996), into whose brains the drive to narrativize our lives appears to be hard-wired. "Conscious mental life," insists well-known sociobiologist, Edmund O. Wilson (2014), "is a constant review of stories experienced in the past and competing stories invented for the future" (p. 51). "Our minds," he writes, "consist of storytelling" (p. 51).

Narrative knowing, narrative reasoning, narrative processing, narrative imagination - these are core kinds of cognition. Jerome Bruner, a leader in the field of cognitive science whose pioneering impact is regularly cited by narrative psychologists, has distinguished, for instance, between "two modes of thought," namely "logical or paradigmatic thought" and "narrative thought" (1986). Logical thought is what we prize so much in science or philosophy or the law, and which we program computers to excel at and hound students to become better at. On the other hand, narrative thought, which has its own brand of logic - "story logic," one source calls it (Herman, 2002) - is what all of us, philosopher and poet alike, engage in every day. Yet we engage in it so unthinkingly, as it were, that we scarcely notice it at all. My phrase for it is "narrative intelligence" (Randall, 1999), something I see as not simply one of the multiple intelligences of which we are said to be capable (Gardner, 1990), but a form of intelligence so central to who we are as human beings that human life as we know it would be inconceivable without it.

I'm speaking of the capacity to formulate stories, big and little, to make sense of the events of our lives, and the companion capacity to communicate with others about those events in ways that make sense to them. Obviously, some people are particularly proficient in the practice of both. Novelists or playwrights, for instance, come immediately to mind. So, too, do comedians or journalists, anyone whose work revolves around telling stories; or - in the case of detectives - piecing stories together so that they can settle on "whodunit." But all of us, I would argue, possess narrative intelligence to some degree or other and, with it, are forever storying the stuff of our lives - though by no means all of it.

Insofar as memory - in particular, autobiographical memory (memory for episodes and events in our lives) as opposed to semantic memory (memory for information) or procedural memory (memory for how to do things) - possesses a narrative dimension, we obviously don't have memories, and thus stories, for every part of our lives. Quite the contrary, in fact. In the words of writer Richard Stone (1996), "relatively little of our lives is ever storied." Instead, "most of our experiences and perceptions flow into the amorphous black hole that we call our past, never to be recalled, reflected on, or evaluated." In short, many of our memories are anomalies.

Unless we suffer from hyperthymestic syndrome, a rare neurological disorder in which we lack the capacity to forget (Price, 2008), we don't typically remember every single time that we've ridden in a cab, to take one simple example. Instead, when we think about "riding in a cab" we zero in on that one terrifying time when we narrowly missed colliding with a truck because the driver kept swivelling his head around to talk to us. Arbitrary and biased in its ways, memory is notoriously selective. We tend to remember the exceptions to the rule, the departures from the norm. We remember what, for whatever reasons, we can't forget. And what we remember is rarely the straightforward, unredacted facts, recalled in their entirety, but an edited, embellished, puffed up or pared down version thereof. An amalgam of fiction and fact, autobiographical memory is ultimately a matter of "faction." And taken together, for better or for worse, these factions are integral to our identity, to the work of creative non-fiction that we experience as our "self." Put simply, we understand who we *are* in terms of stories, not statistics.

When someone asks us to tell them a bit about ourselves, we don't typically list off a set of facts and figures about our height or weight, our shoe size or age, but rather some sort of narrative, however abbreviated, about our lives. "Well, I was born at a very young age, grew up in rural New Brunswick, went to school in the States, worked as a minister for many years, and then become a gerontologist, so here I am. What about you?" In other words, we give them some sort of *story* about ourselves, one that we make short or long, thick or thin, depending on the time available to us, or what their attention span appears to be, or how interested we reckon they are in the first place.

The instinct to think of our lives in storied terms is so engrained in us that we quite naturally engage in *story-talk*. In other words, besides the familiar expression, *the story of my life*, numerous phrases - leastwise, in English - can sprinkle our everyday speech; phrases that arise from what psychologist Theodore Sarbin calls the "narrative root metaphor" (1986). Asked how things are going for us by a fellow customer at the coffee shop, we answer by saying ... *the same old story*. We go through a major life-change and inform our friends that we've *turned over a new leaf*, or opened *a new chapter*. When our friends see things much the same way we do, we say *we're on the same page*. One friend in particular we dub a *drama queen* behind her back, while an acquaintance who thinks too highly of himself we speak of as *a legend in his own mind*. Of someone who seems especially transparent, we say that we can *read her like a book*, with she herself insisting that we can ask her any question that we wish because ... *my life is an open book*.

IDENTITY AND NARRATIVE

From the introductory course in psychology that we may have taken in university, we have heard of Erik Erikson (1963) and his eight stages of psychosocial development, especially his concept of "identity" - from which we get the iconic concept of *identity crisis*. Building on Erikson's ideas, narrative psychologist, Dan McAdams (2001), sees identity as unquestionably a narrative construction. "*Identity*," he insists, however, "*is a life story*" (p. 643; emphasis McAdams'). In other words, it is "an internalized and evolving narrative of the self" - elsewhere he says "personal myth," or one could even say "guiding fiction" - that "binds together many different aspects of the self to confer upon a life some degree of unity, purpose, and meaning" (p. 643). But this identity-narrative connection, this self-story link, is anything but straightforward, for there's lots going on within it.

For one thing, like the average novel, a lifestory is composed of multiple narrative strands, multiple storylines. The writer Alex Haley, author of the novel *Roots*, made the comment in an interview once that "every time an old person dies it's like a library burns down." In the library of everyone of us, surely countless stories are stored away, and stories of several types. There are short stories about what we did last evening and there are long ones about our first marriage, or about the trials we endured to finish our degree. There are very general stories about good times we've had, hunting or fishing, and highly specific stories about the one time that we hooked onto a salmon. There are stories we can tell about ourselves alone and stories that are about others as much as us. We have stories of the past, but also stories of the future; stories of what might have been and stories of what might still be; stories of our past and future alike that are "counterfactual" in nature (Ferguson, 1997). We have stories rumbling around inside of us that we scarcely know *how* to tell - secret stories, dark stories, toxic stories. But we also have stories that we can trot out at the drop of a hat: "signature stories," you might call them - stories that we're more than happy to share with others in order to give them a sense of who we are and the more salient of our life's events (Kenyon & Randall, 1997, pp. 46-49). One of my own, for example, is about being in an iron lung for two weeks at the age of two, a story that I'll say more about toward the end of the book.

Then, there are broadly identifiable chapters - about our childhood, our days in university, our first full-time job, and so forth - as well as specific sub-plots which can span long stretches of years - about our life as a son, as a sibling, as a sports fan or a spouse. And of course these chapters and subplots, these storylines, can overlap. Yet each one constitutes its own unique angle on our life story as a whole. As for our self itself - both the self that tells and the self that is told about - it is a complex concept in its own right, more "dialogical" (Hermans,

2000) than unitary in nature. As one writer wisely notes, "there are many stories of Self to tell, and many selves to tell them" (Eakin, 1999, p. xi).

The identity-story connection is complicated all the more, of course, because the gendered dimension is always at play. Research shows, for instance, that girls and women tell stories about the events of their lives that tend to be more detailed, more layered, and more emotionally nuanced than those that boys and men are socialized to recount (see, e.g., Fivush, 1994). For males are more likely to be coached not to embellish but to keep things simple, to stick to the facts. In her book *Composing A Life*, anthropologist Mary Catherine Bateson (1989) suggests a similar trend. Men have traditionally tried to script their lives, she says, according to "a model of single-track ambition" (p. 15), while for women - with lives that accommodate multiple tasks and multiple roles - the focus of composing a life is much more on "the fluid, the protean, the improvisatory" (p. 4). These sorts of differences in self-storying can have major implications in terms of the inner resources, and therefore the resilience, that members of each gender bring to the challenges of later life. This is a theme that I'll come back to later on, for I believe it can play a real - if un-looked-at - role in why women routinely live longer than men. This leads me to say a few words about two concepts that are particularly important in this regard: *storyworld* and *storying style*.

In my 20s and 30s I was a great fan of the English author, Graham Greene, not just his novels, like *The Power and the Glory* or *The End of the Affair*, but his short stories, too. For reasons I can't quite explain, they spoke to me. They took me to a place inside of myself, and to a range of feelings, that no other writer could. One reviewer noted, however, that though the plots and characters vary from one work to the next, the world of themes and moods that Greene's readers are ushered into is familiar across the board. The reviewer's word for it was "Greeneland." The same can be said, of course, for the works of other authors too, whether Hemingway or Atwood, Alice Munro or Stephen King - it matters not. It's the peculiar "feel" that their work possesses, the atmosphere that radiates around it. It's the unique kind of comfort that we derive from the worlds such writers create, and what keeps us reading what they write, compelling us upon occasion to stand in line for hours outside the bookstore awaiting the release of their latest work.

Something similar could be claimed for each of us, however. Our chums can sometimes chastise us for living in our own little world. But it's true. Each of us lives in our own little world, our own little *story*world, that is. Supporting this way of looking at things, English professor-turned-psychotherapist, William Bridges (1980), proposes, for instance, that "we are like stories that are slowly unfolding according to our own inner theme and plot" (p. 71). This explains something of the power that our own stories can have on our psyche and thus how hard it can be for us to make major change. "Each of us resists change," says Bridges, "because a story is a self-coherent world with its own kind of immune system" (p. 71).

The point here is that getting to know someone new is not just a matter of learning their likes and dislikes or getting clear on the principal events of their life history to date. It is a matter of trying to crawl inside (however vicariously) their unique way of storying their lives. And closely related to a person's storyworld, perhaps its most distinguishing feature, is the unique angle from which they look at what's going on in their lives, the distinct sort of perspective or voice, or more accurately the *genre*, according to which they typically interpret things: tragic, comic, romantic, ironic, satirical, and so forth.
McAdams calls this our characteristic "narrative tone," and speaks of it as "ranging from blissful optimism to biting negativism" (1996, p. 136). I call it our *storying style* (Randall, 1995/2014, pp. 308-328).

The concept of storying style takes in the way that people tend to talk about what's happening in their lives - whether tersely or obtusely, ironically or matter-of-fact, in a higgledy-piggledy, self-interrupting manner or a one-thought-at-a-time, easy to follow one, with nice, neat narrative arcs, and so on and so forth, with all sorts of possibilities in between. And it also takes in how people portray themselves amidst their lives. An example from my own life might illustrate what I mean.

In the years leading up to his death at 98, I would visit my father daily at the retirement home where we transferred him after my mother and I could no longer care for him without costly round-the-clock help. Being a good narrative gerontologist, I would ask him to tell me (yet again!) some of the more engaging stories from his life, stories that were topmost in his memory, stories that he in fact quite *liked* to tell - his signature stories, if you will. I knew these would re-invigorate his sense of identity and get him feeling positive about himself again, good about his life overall. It struck me one day, however, that in almost every story I remembered him telling me over the years, from whatever period of his life, he would position himself vis-à-vis the other characters in his tale as the smart kid, as the one who knew how to deal with the bullies on the playground, as the one who alone could tell what needed saying or doing in a given situation. To be fair, he didn't come across in a braggartly manner, but humbly almost. Yet, with a robust sense of narrative agency overall, he very much cast himself as the hero within his own storyworld.

The same moment I realized this, it struck me that my own storying style was markedly different, just the opposite in fact. Many of the stories that I tell others about myself, many of my signature stories, are basically *on* myself. The stories that stand out most from my library across the years are those in which I come out looking like the dummy, the loser, the fool; not the champ, but the chump. Why this is the case, I don't have a ready answer, though a therapist might. Perhaps I position myself in relation to the others in my stories in a one-down rather than one-up manner because I want my listeners to *like* me, because I don't want them to think that I think I'm better than them. Whatever the reason, I offer this difference between my father and me as an example of how we each have a distinctive storying style that figures in one way or another, often hugely, in the narrative identity in terms of which we live.

Complicating the self-story link still further, our stories are intertwined inside of us with other stories too. There can be stories within stories, in other words, stories beneath stories, stories between the lines, back stories or shadow stories behind our actions and reactions, our emotions and opinions - stories we don't quite know *how* to tell, or who to tell them to. There are untold stories that are tied to the lines on our faces, the looks in our eyes, our postures and gestures, the sighs we breathe when no one is near. For our stories are not just in our heads or hearts but also in our bodies. In the words of writer, Carolyn Myss (1996), "our bodies contain our histories;" in effect, "biography becomes biology" (p. 40).

Many of our stories - short or long, past or future, big or small - are entwined, of course, with the stories of others. Narratively speaking, none of us is an island. I can't tell my own story without at some point telling some portion of my father's story or my sister's, or at least the portion of their stories (as perceived by me) that pertains to mine. And where my story begins and that of my partner ends is impossible to state, for all manner of "we-stories" have sprung up between us that bind our lives together (Singer & Skerrett, 2014). As William Bridges (1980) wryly observes: "to become a couple is to agree implicitly to live in terms of another person's story, although," he adds impishly, "it sometimes takes time to get the part down really well" (p. 71).

As I'll be discussing more fully next chapter, our stories are also continually changing - as new events are added, new subplots being woven in, new characters entering the scene and old ones exiting stage left, new themes being seeded, new meanings sprouting up. At least in the central decades of our life, the plot as a whole is thus thickening all the more, whether for better or for worse. For the stories in our libraries, particularly the overarching ones in terms of which we tell ourselves and others who we are, can become stunted, stifled, distorted, or otherwise dysfunctional. Once more, our stories are not innocent. In short, "some stories are better than others" (McAdams, 2008, p. 247) and, as I've implied already with my notion of "a good strong story," may help us live longer, healthier lives. In the words of pastoral theologian, Janet Ruffing (2011), "it matters how we tell the story" (pp. 93-130).

I'll return to this line of thinking in Chapter 5 when I look into the narrative challenges that can face us in later life. Later life is a time when, for an assortment of reasons, our storyworld can start to narrow in - or at least, what Bruner (1986) calls the "landscape of action" (p. 14), namely the realm of events. However, the "landscape of consciousness" - the realm of awareness, of interpretation, of narrating and meaning-making - can expand indefinitely within us. Similarly, the emotional complexity of our lives can intensify as well, insofar as it, in turn, is bound up with age-related changes in our autobiographical memory, our autobiographical reasoning, our sense of narrative identity, and our capacity for post-formal thought. The narrative complexity of our emotions is yet one more topic on the frontier edge of narrative research, one more rabbit hole to wander down. In all, then, the whole identity-narrative connection raises a multitude of questions to bear in mind. As one of my students astutely noted in the journal that she kept for my course on Narrative Gerontology, "there's nothing simple about a life story!"

By way of wrapping up, a few further points are worth making to support the idea at the heart of this chapter, namely that later life is "the narrative phase par excellence" (Freeman, 1997, p. 394).

LATER LIFE AS THE NARRATIVE PHASE

Narrative psychologists have noted that negative life-events, such as illness, loss, or trauma, tend to require of us more narrative activity to make sense of them. They "demand more storytelling work" (McAdams, 2008, p. 253), which helps to explain why positive events, however pleasurable they may be, can be strangely less easy to bring to mind. It's uncanny, for example, how readily we can recall the more embarrassing moments in our lives, all the times when things went wrong, yet have great difficulty recalling the times when things went right. But is this so surprising? A story that had a happy beginning, a happy ending, *and* a happy middle would not make much of a story. As Bruner (1999) tells us, a tale needs "trouble" (p. 8). Something needs to go wrong so that the plot can kick into gear and make things right (more or less) in the end. With the stresses and difficulties - the Trouble - that aging can bring, it too, in general, I suggest, demands more storytelling work: to make sense of what's going on; to square our often more limited life and more threatened self in the present with the fuller life and feistier self that may have characterized our past.

It's been said as well that, because of this Trouble, later life presents us with "a crisis of meaning" (Missine, 2003, p. 113), not unlike the crisis of *identity* that Erikson claims confronts us in adolescence. We may find ourselves wondering ... "who am I, now that I am no longer gainfully employed, now that I can no longer contribute to society like I did in the past, now that I can no longer do my fair share of work in the kitchen or the yard?" Again, the need for meaning is linked to the need for narrative - for narrative thought, that is, more than logical thought. We tell stories to make sense of our lives, therefore the more besieged our lives become by the challenges of aging, the more the need to tell our stories is likely to grow.

Conveniently, changes in our aging brains themselves - specifically better cooperation between left and right hemispheres - help to heighten this narrative urge, says gerontologist, Gene Cohen (2005). They help to intensify the "autobiographical drive" (p. 23) - the drive to get our stories out or down, for the sake not just of our children or whomever else will hear us and heed, but of ourselves as well, for the sake of our sanity, our self-worth. Put another way, there are unique developmental tasks that await us in later life, part of the philosophic homework that I've mentioned already, and linked to these tasks are unique developmental challenges. And these tasks and challenges, I'm saying, are primarily *narrative* in nature. They concern the stories we *are*, and how, even in our latter years, those stories continue to unfold.

PART II

Narrative Development in Later Life

CHAPTER 4
Narrative Development and the Tasks of Later Life

[T]here is little of greater importance to each of us than gaining a perspective on our own life story, to find, clarify, and deepen meaning in the accumulated experience of a lifetime.
- James Birren & Donna Deutchman (1991, p. 1)

A growing, deepening, knitting together of your life, a consciousness of what you've lived needing to come together in a whole picture, as if you have to integrate your whole life to prepare for the sloughing off of the body, as if in age the soul is getting ready to take off – the big adventure.
- Suzanne Wagner (cited in Friedan, 1993, p. 575)

I suggested a while back that we can envision our lives as vast, ever-changing narrative worlds that we're squarely in the middle of, as author (or co-author), narrator, protagonist, editor, and reader more or less at once, making them up as we go along - always from the inside. In Anton Boisen's (1936) classic phrase, we are "living human documents." My way of capturing this somewhat odd way of looking at things is to speak of the *novelty* of our lives (Randall, 1999). But novels possess a dynamic dimension. Like any story, they have to go somewhere. Otherwise, we lose interest fairly soon. It is this dynamic dimension that I want to turn to now as I consider the idea of narrative development.

OUR CHANGING STORYWORLDS

While it's true that we each live in our own little storyworld, that world is far from static. It is continually changing. To illustrate this otherwise obvious point, I have three photos of myself at different stages in my life that I like showing in presentations that I make on narrative gerontology. In one of them, I'm posing with my parents and sisters at the dining room table in the house I had just purchased, back in 1998, three years after coming to St. Thomas University to teach gerontology. In another, I'm with my mother and my sister, Donna, standing in the sanctuary of the church that I was serving at the time, in the village of Creemore, Ontario, my clerical collar visible beneath my blue suit and a poppy pinned to my lapel, since it was Remembrance Day Sunday. This would have been in 1989, just as I was exiting my ministerial career and embarking on the doctoral studies that led to the career that I've been pursuing ever since.

In the third photo, a faded little black and white, I'm somewhere around 7 or 8 and standing, arms akimbo, in front of Al Knowlton's General Store in my hometown of Harvey Station. I have this strange smirk on my face, however. Why might that be?, I wonder, as I stare at this image from a day in my life of which, truth be told, I have no recollection at all. What was behind my expression? Was I mad? Was I scared? Was I impatient, annoyed with whoever was taking my picture because they were ... taking my picture? Or did I badly need to pee? And what sort of storyworld did I see myself living in the middle of on that sunny summer day in my young little life, assuming I saw my life in "story" terms at all?

Emptying the apartment where my parents had lived before moving to the facility where my mother, in fact, still resides, I stumbled upon something that gave me an endearing glimpse into the things that were apparently important to me at the time. It was a photocopy of a letter that I had typed (yes, typed!) to family friends, Ora and Sheldon, on the occasion of my eighth birthday. A classic kinkeeper in our family, my mother was a stickler for writing our bread-and-butter letters to thank Aunt so-and-so or Uncle whats-his-name for the socks or hankies that they'd sent us for Christmas, as soon as possible thereafter, with effusive phrases like "they're the most wonderful socks I've ever had!" The letter goes like this:

Dec. 1, 1958

Dear Ora and Sheldon,

I thank you an awful lot for the gun and holster and 43 bullets. It is a real good gun. You can flash draw. Daddy said we could try practising at Grammy's [his mother-in-law's] pictures. You know on TV that show 'Have Gun Will Travel'? I think it is his pair of guns. I don't really know if it is his. I suppose you got it when you were in New York. I wonder if you counted the bullets. Well, I did. There are 43 bullets.

Well, I must go now. Write to me soon.

Your friend

Billy

In reading this little letter, and looking at this picture, or indeed at any pictures from my past that are stashed in boxes at the back of my closet, the question that haunts me is: How has my story of "me" evolved from one stage of my life to the next? How am I the same and how am I different? I'm certainly not the first to puzzle about such questions. In an essay entitled simply "Life as Narrative," considered by connoisseurs of narrative ideas to be seminal in nature, Bruner (1987) writes that he "cannot imagine a more important psychological research project than one that addresses itself to the 'development of autobiography';" in other words, "how our way of telling about ourselves changes, and how these accounts come to take control of our ways of life" (p. 12). This notion of autobiographical development, or more broadly narrative development, has not been taken nearly as seriously by researchers on aging as you might expect. As I say, biographical aging has made it onto the radar of academic gerontology only rather recently, and even then it is far from being the central focus of attention. Which is all the more reason it behoves us to make it our focus here.

In short, our stories are not stationary. They thicken with time, or at the very least, they change. When I try to imagine, for example, what was happening in my life at each previous stage - 1998, 1989, 1958 - I realize that my storyworld has obviously broadened in scope. More events have occurred, more milestones been passed, and more challenges and achievements added: graduating from high school, trundling off to college, attending seminary, surviving my first two parishes, then returning to university and clambering up the academic ladder. And with these experiences, new chapters have opened up, new subplots been introduced (and with them new tensions), new themes woven in, new episodes laid down in memory, and new characters - colleagues, students, partners, friends - enriching the story as a whole, or if not enriching it then certainly expanding it, complicating the mix. For this reason, as psychologist Donald Polkinghorne (1988) describes the situation in his masterful book, *Narrative Knowing and the Human Sciences*, "we are constantly having to revise the plot as new events are added to our lives" (p. 150). We are constantly having to re-evaluate what our story is, in other words. We are constantly re-storying.

This need we feel to revise the plot, whether consciously or (more likely) not, points to an aspect of narrative development that makes things additionally intriguing as far as aging is concerned. Linguistic scholar, Charlotte Linde (1993), notes in her book *Life Stories: The Quest for Coherence* that the stories we weave and re-weave about our lives are not just structurally open, in terms of the events that they comprise, which are of course forever being added to. They are "interpretively open" (p. 31), too. We tell stories to make sense of events, that is, but as time goes by we tend to tell those stories in different ways, and, in consequence, make different sense.

As for the tale I told my chums the next day at school about getting the gun with 43 bullets for my birthday, I probably told it quite differently to my dorm-mates ten years later in college - assuming I remembered it at all. And when I tell it now, it's different again. Not only do I get a chuckle out of it for how cute I was to write that little letter at all, but I interpret its significance in quite different ways within the ever-thickening context of the life that I've lived since that day I turned 8. It's not just that I'm nostalgic for the much simpler life that (as I look back now) I was leading at the time, but I find myself enjoying an ironic affection for the several other selves that I've since gone on to be.

For such reasons, and as most older adults have at some point no doubt felt, our understanding of the past can shift within us in ever-so subtle ways, surprising us, even overwhelming us, with how, unbeknownst to us, our life has bulked up inside of us across the years. In the words of artist Anne Truitt (1987), "my life has accumulated behind my own back while I was living it" (p. 17). Going one step further, May Sarton (1981), best known for the journals that she published in her later years, remarks how "the past is always changing, is never static, never 'placed' forever like a book on a shelf. As we grow and change," she says, "we understand things in new ways" (p. 95). As life goes on," she writes in another place,"it becomes more intense because there are tremendous numbers of associations and so many memories" (Sarton, 1977, p. 231).

Put simply, while the real past is fixed - what happened, happened, and can't be changed - the remembered past is fluid. As Sarton says, we understand things in new ways. New meanings can always be gleaned from old tales (Chandler & Ray, 2002). And those meanings accrue. They build on one another, grow out of one another. As happens when reading a novel, with the impact of the story intensifying within us from beginning to end, "the meaning of the past [is] something that develops throughout life" (Charmé, 1984, p. 40).

On the physical or biological level, there appears to be a built-in limit to how old we can get, with 120 years, give or take, as the maximum age we seem capable of attaining. But on a biographical or narrative level, there is no limit whatsoever to how old we can *grow*. Put another way, just as any novel worth its salt leaves us with no end of things to ponder or discuss, there is no intrinsic end to our narrative development. It is open-ended. Or as I suggested back in Chapter 2, our own lifestories possess endless parabolic potential.

My father was a great one for poetry. Remembering poems, word for word, had been central to his school curriculum growing up. He delighted in regaling us with little rhymes like ... *Backward turn backward, oh time in thy flight, and make me a boy again just for tonight.* Or ... *It wasn't the cough that finished him off, but the coffin they carried him off in.* One of his favourites was Wordsworth's poem about the daffodils. The two of us would compete with each other to recall each line of it in order. A favourite, as well, was "The Chambered Nautilius" by Oliver Wendell Holmes (2005/1895). The older he got, the more he loved reciting it. Perhaps it was for the sense of open-endedness it conveys, for the hope at its heart, for the metaphor it offers of the sequence of storyworlds that we can move into and out of as we age; for the image of the spiral - not circular but spiral - dynamics of spiritual development, and of narrative development too:

> *Build thee more stately mansions,*
> *O my soul,*
> *As the swift seasons roll!*
> *Leave thy low-vaulted past!*
> *Let each new temple,*
> *Nobler than the last,*
> *Shut thee from heaven with a dome more vast,*
> *Till thou at length art free,*
> *Leaving thine outgrown shell by life's unresting sea.*

STAGES OF NARRATIVE DEVELOPMENT

I've mentioned already the work of developmental psychologist, Dan McAdams. As developmentalists are prone to do, McAdams (1996) has proposed a broad set of stages according to which autobiographical development, or *narrative development*, occurs. Before talking about the unique developmental tasks of later life, which I'll be stressing are narrative tasks at heart, I'd like to sketch the three he has in mind. Corresponding roughly to the beginning-middle-end structure that we associate with a story, they are: the *pre-mythic* stage, the *mythic* stage, and the *post-mythic* stage.

The pre-mythic stage runs from infancy through early childhood and into our pre-teen years. During it, he says, we are unwittingly "gathering material" (pp. 136-138) - little episodes and adventures, that is - for what will in due course get incorporated into the story, or myth, of our life that we'll begin more consciously to patch together for ourselves in the mythic stage. My iron lung story would be a case in point, and possibly the gun and holster story too, except that, apart from the photocopied letter that I only just found, I have no memory of it whatsoever. The key is that our gathering of material often happens beneath the radar of conscious awareness.

In the mythic stage, which for McAdams commences in earnest with the advent of adolescence, we begin to draw on some of this memory material that we've been quietly collecting and start assembling a coherent storyline about our lives - past, present, and future. The key, though, is that it is *our* narrative of us, not Mommy's or Daddy's or our teacher's or anyone else's.
Rather, we're at last assuming narrative responsibility for our lives, deferring less and less to the authority of others. This can be a tumultuous phase for others to put up with, however - for parents and siblings, for sure - because, on top of the usual upheavals that puberty brings (changing bodies, changing hormones), our autobiographical consciousness is awakening in ways that it hasn't been before. We're officially "beginning the story" (p. 138), tackling head-on the question of our own unique identity, not defaulting to someone else's story about us that we've internalized as true - a condition that has been referred to as "identity foreclosure" (see Marcia & Josselson, 2013, p. 620f), which is linked to "*narrative* foreclosure" (Freeman, 2000), a concept I'll come back to next chapter.

As we shift from adolescence into adulthood, says McAdams (1996), we are continually "expanding the story" (p. 140). Narratively speaking, there can be loads of activity on multiple fronts: family, marriage, children, career. As I say, more episodes are being added, more chapters opening up, more themes emerging, more characters coming and going. The plot is thickening all the while. Our storyworld reflects ever more "differentiation," one of six criteria that McAdams associates with "a good life story" (2001, p. 663). Others include coherence, credibility, reconciliation, generative integration, and above all, openness: concepts I'll return to later. But while steadily expanding the story, we can also, in so-called mid-life, often just beneath the surface, engage in a measure of re-storying too, of "revising the plot," as Polkinghorne would put it. By this I mean, critiquing the identity-narrative that we began fashioning for ourselves in adolescence but never stepped back from to ask how fairly it reflected who we are now, or who we feel ourselves becoming. The point is that identity-work is never complete. It continues all life long, and shake-ups in our stories can occur at any time.

When I left full-time ministry in my late 30s, I was involved in some major re-storying of my own. I recall walking the streets of Toronto evening after evening in the first few months of what was, for me, a dramatic life-transition, both professionally and personally. Walking, walking, and more walking, trying to clear my head, until eventually I sought out a counsellor to help me unpack the baggage that my psyche had acquired from that ten-year, all-consuming chapter when my identity as "me" - and not "minister" - was all but buried.

As for the post-mythic stage, which begins at no specific age, though typically as we move into our 50s and 60s, our identity-work doesn't cease, but it does tend to shift in subtle though important ways, as does our orientation toward time. Not in all cases, of course, but generally speaking, looking ahead to the future pre-occupies us less than looking back upon the past. Also, whereas the plot of our story was thickening throughout the mythic stage, a measure of thinning may begin to occur. We retire from our job or profession, our friends and family move away or pass away, our mobility is compromised, we transition from our home-home to a nursing home, and our storyworld invariably narrows in. Or at least the outward aspect of it does, the landscape of action that a story entails. Once again, the landscape of action concerns the characters, the setting, and the events, or what *happens* in the story: the action. The landscape of consciousness, on the other hand, concerns what people *think* of what happens. It concerns what happens in characters' minds, what the narrator sees and feels, what the author, behind the scenes, is seeking to say through the themes around which the story revolves. And it concerns what happens in our minds as readers or listeners or viewers. It's in this landscape of consciousness - which is to say, the *inside* of aging - where the developmental tasks unique to later life come most into play.

THE THIRTEEN R'S OF LATER LIFE

The lad obsessed with how many bullets he'd received was being schooled each day in the proverbial *Three R's* - of Readin', 'Ritin', and 'Rithmetic. The developmental tasks that I'll be looking into now, all of them inter-related, can be thought of as *The Thirteen R's* of later life.

The term "developmental tasks" refers to those things we need to master, or are expected by society to master, in order to advance in our evolution as individuals. Learning to walk and talk and go to the toilet on our own are the sorts of tasks to be mastered when we're one or two. But each subsequent stage of life will have tasks appropriate to it in turn. Later life is no exception, except that the tasks it assigns us are more subtle, more internal, or as I've said before, more philosophical in nature. They are bound up with the homework I've been referring to from the start and, as such, are more narrative in nature as well. I can't stress this enough. These tasks - and, admittedly, "task" may be too strong a term - are inner, not outer, in essence. I see them as welling up organically within us, nudging us gently from inside, not imposed upon us from without, like items on a To Do list to be checked off one by one when completed. We can resist these nudgings, to be sure - repressing them, ignoring them, or otherwise inuring ourselves to them through incessant activity or addictive behaviour. But they will be happening within us all the same.

Erik Erikson (1963) has argued that what we need to do to achieve "ego integrity" in the last of his eight stages of psychosocial development is to engage in a process of life

review (see Butler, 1963). Though researchers have shown that this need is not something all of us equally or automatically experience, as Erikson originally assumed (see Wink & Schiff, 2002), life review is a complex cognitive-emotional process. Whether spontaneously and semi-consciously or in a structured, intentional manner, it involves stepping back from the lives that we have lived and taking stock of all that we have been and done, or at least as much of it as we can bring to mind. It involves reflecting on the experiences we have accumulated across the years - the hurts and regrets, the accomplishments and achievements - and hopefully arriving at a sense of acceptance that, all things considered, our life has been worthwhile. And, with Erikson's concept of "generativity" in mind, it hopefully results in us feeling that we have made a positive contribution, however modest it might be, to the welfare of our family, our community, our world (Kotre, 1984).

In his book, *Hindsight: The Promise and Peril of Looking Backward*, Mark Freeman (2010) uses the term "narrative **reflection**" rather than review. For him, though, it is similar, and similarly essential for psychological development and moral development alike. Not just in later life, of course, but at any point along the way - a graduation, a wedding, a milestone of any sort: whenever we pause to take the long view of the life we've lived to date. Our growth as persons in a forward direction, toward deepened self-understanding and self-acceptance, is intimately linked, says Freeman, to reflecting back over our lives as a whole, a process that Israeli scholar, Gabriela Spector-Mersel (2017) calls "big story narrative reflection." It is linked to taking the long view of our lives. For just as the significance of certain events in a story can only be grasped as we near The End, there are certain experiences that we can only understand, patterns we can only make out, themes we can only discern, from the vantage point in space and time that later life affords. Simply put, it is linked to thinking about things, making sense of things, reasoning about things, to "autobiographical **reasoning**" (Habermas, 2010) - yet another R. All of these (reviewing, reflecting, reasoning) are involved, of course, in organizations like Alcoholics Anonymous, which require members in the fifth of their 12-step programs to make "a searching and fearless moral inventory" of their lives.

Anthropologist Barbara Myerhoff (1992) uses another term for this business of reviewing, reflecting, and reasoning. She calls it **re-membering** our lives, with a hyphen placed deliberately between the "re" and the "membering." By this she means, basically, connecting the scattered corners of our past and experiencing some measure of psychic wholeness in the process - or, as Erikson would day, of ego integrity. **Re-assembling** might be a comparable term to use; re-assembling our sense of self as we navigate the tricky transition into the second half of life, with the various losses (of mobility, of autonomy, of pain-free living) that can accompany it. I think of re-assembling and re-membering as a matter of pulling ourselves together. *Pull yourself together*, our friends may have urged us at one point or other. The more I age, the more I feel the urge to do the same.

The first thing I'd like to do on the day that I officially retire, for instance, is to clear away the tables and chairs from a classroom on campus and empty out onto its floor all of the photographs that I talked about above, plus my diaries and journals, and all the cards and letters folks have kindly sent me through the years, and that I've felt the need to keep. I'm thinking, in particular, of the notes that students have left in my mailbox at Convocation time or Christmastime, or sent me as an email, thanking me for this and that, and generally assuring me that I've affected their lives for the better. When at last I've strewn all this stuff on the floor and stepped back to survey it, I'm hoping that I'll experience a surge of amazement at how varied, valued, and vast my life has really been. Thus, I imagine, will commence in earnest the process of pulling that life together in my heart.

Experts in **reminiscence** - yet another R - would call this *integrative* reminiscence, or even dynamic reminiscence, to distinguish it from, say, *instrumental* reminiscence, which is where we use our memories of how we've handled things in the past to help us deal with comparable things in the present. Or from *transmissive* reminiscence, where we recount what things were like in the past in order to transmit knowledge or values that can enlighten others in the present. Or certainly from *escapist* reminiscence, where we harken back wistfully to "the good old days" because we find the present so troubling or so boring by comparison. Or *obsessive* reminiscence, where we are fixated on some negative experience that happened years ago and keep going over it and over it in our minds, or with anyone willing to listen (see Wong, 1995).

Here, then, are a few more R's to keep in mind regarding the developmental tasks - the narrative tasks - that later life assigns us. In an article entitled "Creating a Life Story," gerontologist Peter Coleman (1999), who has devoted much of his research to understanding the psychic bruises that veterans can carry with them in the wake of war, writes about "the task of **reconciliation**." By this he means incorporating into our story not just the good of our lives but, as much as possible, the bad and the ugly as well: the troubles, tragedies, and traumas that have resisted assimilation into our sense of self. I would add to this that it also means to integrate into our story the various selves we might have been, or might still be; the "possible selves" (Markus & Nurius, 1986) in our past and future alike; the "unlived lives" (Alheit, 1995, p. 65) that each of us carries around inside of us - not thereby to be crippled with regret, which is always a possibility, of course, but to be thickened with an awareness of our internal complexity and depth. As I noted earlier, McAdams (2001) lists "reconciliation" as one of six criteria for a "good life story" (p. 663). He admits, though, that it is "one of the most challenging tasks in the making of life stories, especially in midlife and beyond" (p. 664)

- a point worth recalling as we seek to assist older adults with aging in-depth, to say nothing of aging in-depth ourselves.

In his book, *The Redemptive Self*, McAdams (2006) writes of the importance of **redeeming** the events of our lives, which is to say finding the positive within the negative, the learning beyond the loss, the truth beneath the tragic. In a similar vein, Rabbi Schacter-Shalomi writes about **re-contextualizing** past experiences in light of our life trajectory overall (Schacter-Shalomi & Miller, 1995, p. 94). In the process, he suggests, we will experience a diminishing of the regret or embarrassment that we might otherwise feel. Things that seemed pointless or horrid at the time they took place can be seen, in their own unique way, as essential to our becoming who we've become. We will come full circle in our understanding of their significance, the circle being more of a spiral, however, for the place we come back around to is further along on our developmental path, with a wider panorama available to us. We could speak of this process not just as re-contextualizing but as **re-genre-ating**. Here, the work of gerontologist, Harry Berman (1994) is worth citing.

In researching the role that keeping a journal can play in our personal development in later life, Berman - who sees humans as "self-interpreting animals" (p. 21) and claims that we need a "hermeneutical gerontology" (p. xxiv) - touches on the narrative openness that this sort of reflection can foster, the re-storying to which it can lead, enabling us to see our lives in novel ways. As our "horizon of self-understanding shifts," he says, "it may become apparent that we were not in the middle of the story we thought we were in the middle of. Perhaps we thought our life was a tragedy and all along, unbeknownst to us, it was a romance. Or perhaps we thought our life was almost over," Berman observes, "at least in terms of the future holding anything new, and it turned out there was a lot more to it" (p. 180). In such cases, the term *post*-mythic may be the wrong one to use. For a fresh myth might well be in the works, not unlike

Gene Cohen's (2005) vision of the "encore" phase of later life. In words reminiscent of Betty Friedan's (1993) view of "age as adventure," Cohen describes this as "a time when entirely new perspectives on our life can come forth" (p. 82f). Such observations call to mind the quip that makes the rounds sometimes among psychiatrists: *It's never too late to have a happy childhood!*

Other R's to add to the list include **reaping.** In *From Ageing to Sageing*, which advocates for more "spiritual eldering" in our society, Schachter-Shalomi (1995) stresses the need for "life harvesting," namely "gathering in the fruits of a lifetime's experience and enjoying them in old age" (p. 53). Then there is **repairing**: mending fences, making amends, restoring strained relationships wherever possible, or if not, then finding some peace of mind regarding them, some feeling of forgiveness: whether forgiveness of others or forgiveness of ourselves. There is Freeman's term **rewriting**, too; as in the title of his ground-breaking book, *Rewriting The Self: History, Memory, Narrative* (1994).

Then there is **recycling**. By this I mean passing along our portion of wisdom - which really means our *story*, insofar as our wisdom lies within our stories (Randall & Kenyon, 2001) - to those who are younger than us, who hopefully will benefit from the lessons that we've learned across the years. This is a variation on transmissive reminiscence that psychologist John Kotre (1984) refers to as "generative transference" (p. 247). We might call it "generative narration" as well (McAdams, 2001, p. 583). The grander term for those who share their wisdom and stories with others, and a term whose currency I would like to hope can be revived, is the term *Elder*. With his love of telling stories from his life, offering others not just entertainment by means of them but encouragement and guidance as well, I think of my father, for example, as having been an Elder to many.

It's easy to get carried away with alliteration. Going beyond the thirteen that I've mentioned already, other R's to include in the list could be **reframing**, **rehearsing**, and even **ruminescing**, which is a blend of reminiscing and ruminating. Not ruminating in an obsessive sense, however. Rather, the focus at some subliminal level is on the slow questions that have been swirling away amidst our memories, beckoning to us, siren-like, with increasing insistence. Ruminating is what we do when material from our past re-surfaces involuntarily - regurgitates, as it were - and invites us to digest it, to ponder it, afresh. Some of this material may come from periods in our life that have been particularly powerful in shaping our identity; the period, for instance, from our mid-teens to our late 20s (the mythic stage, par excellence), which is typically rich in the formation of memories that we gravitate back to whenever we reminisce; memories of "firsts," for example - first job, first kiss, first marriage, and the like. Researchers who graph the peaks and valleys of memory formation across the years refer to this as the "reminiscence bump" (Neisser & Libby, 2000, p. 318).

And then, conceivably, there is **rejoicing** as well, not so much as a task to be tackled, but as a consequence of coping with the other tasks too. I mean by this rejoicing in our unique *legacy* (Kotre, 1999), whatever we deem that legacy to be, or can be helped by a skilled listener to identify. It could be the children that we've brought into the world, or the contributions, great or small, that we've made to our community, our profession, our world, or to the welfare of others' lives in general - our legacy of *generativity*, that is. For my father, it was all the years of ministry that he practised, all the sermons he delivered, and all the people whose lives he touched in the process, and of course, for him and my mother both, the three of us children. For my sister, Donna, her sense of legacy orbits around her two daughters and the three grandchildren they have given her in turn. For me, not having children of my own, my sense of legacy comes when I consider all of the students whose thinking I've helped to mould, plus the ideas I've shared with the wider world through my various publications.

Legacies can take all manner of forms, from the grand and dramatic to the normal and everyday. One woman who participated in a "narrative care" program at a nursing home near my university - a program I'll say more about in Chapter 8 - was interviewed about the story of her life over a series of sessions. From one session to the next, she kept pen and pad handy so that as things came into her head she could jot them down and thus ensure that they got inserted into her narrative. One thing in particular she couldn't wait to tell the interviewer the next time that they met. On her pad she had scribbled out the phrase: "best dessert-maker EVER!" (Noonan, 2011, p. 363).

What these different R's could be said to concern in common is a process that Beth McKim and I refer to as **reading** our lives (Randall & McKim, 2008). Yet another R, I realize, but if, as I'm suggesting, our lives are inseparable from our *stories* of our lives; if our lives are richly ambiguous texts that we're in the middle of, making them up as we go, then at some point, as Beuchner has advised, it behooves us to "read with open minds the book our life is writing, and learn." This, I submit, is how we strengthen the stories by which we understand our lives, and how we render them more resilient. And I see it as a core developmental task of later life. Giving voice to the sense of integrity - the sense of integration - to which tackling it can lead are these stirring words by Florida Scott-Maxwell (1968) from *The Measure of My Days*:

> *You need only claim the events of your life to make yourself yours. When you truly possess all you have been and done, which may take some time, you are fierce with reality. When at last age has assembled you together, will it not be easy to let it all go, lived, balanced, over?* (p. 40)

CHAPTER 5

Narrative Resilience and the Challenges of Later Life

*Our destinies are opened or closed in terms of
the stories that we construct to understand our experiences.*
- Harry Goolishian (1990)

*We live by stories, we also live in them ...
If we change the stories we live by, quite possibly we change our lives.*
- Ben Oki (cited in King, 2003, p. 153)

I hinted at the outset that the comparatively long lives of both my father (who died at 98) and my sister, Carol (who has made it to 75), have been due in no small part to their having good strong stories. By the phrase "a good strong story" I mean an overall narrative of our lives that is thick and rich and open - openness being one of the core criteria that McAdams (2001) cites as vital for "a good life story" (p. 663f). When I insert the word "strong," however, I don't mean strong as in rigid or inflexible, like some people's self-stories can be - a condition associated with narrative domination or narrative imprisonment, which I'll talk about in a bit. I mean strong as in deep-rooted, far-reaching, and pliant, like the towering pine or spreading oak that bends gracefully to wind and storm. I mean strong as in *resilient*.

NARRATIVE RESILIENCE

The topic of resilience in later life has only quite recently begun to be considered, resilience in children and adolescents having received the majority of research attention to date. Definitions of resilience in later life vary, of course, but I like the fairly straightforward one put forward by writer Mary Pipher (1999). In her book, *Another Country: Negotiating the Emotional Terrain of Elders*, which is based on interviews that she conducted with ordinary older adults, Pipher says this: "Resilience means growing from experience and becoming more who one truly is" (p. 270).

When researchers consider resilience in later life, the factors deemed to feed it are familiar ones in gerontological circles, such as a person's physical health, cognitive status, and financial situation; their level of education, their spiritual or religious involvement, and their network of family and friends (see, e.g., Fry & Keyes, 2010). All of these surely play a role, particularly the spiritual dimension, as Chapter 1, I hope, made clear. But what has been overlooked so far is the narrative dimension. If the developmental tasks of later life are primarily narrative tasks, then what is needed to help us tackle them, we could say, is *narrative* resilience.

Since 2011, a group of us affiliated with the Centre for Interdisciplinary Research on Narrative, or CIRN for short, have been exploring the links between older adults' level of resilience and the sorts of stories that they tell about their lives. The tool we've been using to measure their resilience is the Connor-Davidson Resilience Scale (Connor & Davidson, 2003). The CDRS, as it is known, consists of 25 positively worded statements like "I like challenges" and "I can deal with whatever comes my way," to which you are asked to indicate on a scale from 0 to 4 how well each statement applies to you, where 0 means "not true at all" and 4 means "true nearly all the time." Of the 110 older adults we recruited to fill it out, we chose 15 who scored really high (like 95 to 100 out of 100!), 15 who scored rather low (30 to 50), and 15 who scored in the middle. We then interviewed each of these 45 individuals at length concerning the story of their life overall, with a particular focus on the adversities they experienced along the way.

Our analyses are still ongoing and there are several variables to factor in, not to mention definite limits on what we can confidently conclude. But the over-arching trend that we're uncovering is clear. Those who scored highest on the scale tended to have the richest stories to share. They displayed the most degree of "differentiation" (one of McAdams' six criteria) and the most narrative complexity; as in, multiple stories with lots of detail and dialogue (*I said, she said*, etc.) and numerous themes. And they reflected the strongest degree of narrative agency. That is to say, they exuded a sense of being the protagonist and not the victim within their lives, and also of very much having a story to tell, one that they're quite proud of, in fact. As an example, one woman who scored in the high 90s but who had had all manner of difficulties throughout her life (numerous health concerns, children with disabilities, husbands deceased or divorced) told the interviewer that "I'm hoping to write a book; it would be a trilogy plus."

Those who scored lowest, on the other hand, told comparatively thin stories, with a more pessimistic narrative tone and less narrative agency in general. Plus, harking back to the point I made earlier about gender differences in the narrative-identity connection, they tended to be men. One in particular, at 32 out of 100, was the lowest scorer of all. Despite having a PhD and a successful professional career behind him, he shared a depressingly bleak narrative about his life, one that he recounted in a fatalistic tone (Randall, Baldwin, McKenzie-Mohr, McKim, & Furlong, 2015).

So, then, our preliminary findings would seem to support the hypothesis that it matters a great deal how we tell the story of our lives. This in turn has led us to explore a corollary hypothesis, namely that if we can help people to thicken up their stories, to deepen them and open them out, then we can enhance their self-esteem, intensify their sense of agency, and generally enrich the inner resources that they bring to later life. We can enhance their resilience, in other words. Hence, the value of "narrative care," which is my focus in Part Three. For now, though, I want to segue from the theme of resilience and delve more into the unique sorts of challenges that later life can carry with it.

NARRATIVE CHALLENGES

Just as the tasks of later life are mainly narrative in nature, so, too, are the challenges mainly *narrative* ones. Obviously, aging brings challenges of various kinds. There are practical ones, for instance, like going about our daily activities with arthritis nagging at our joints; medical ones, like living with heart disease or diabetes. Then there are emotional ones, like coping with the loss of a spouse, or friends and family moving on; social ones, like the sense of isolation we can suffer due to vision loss or hearing loss; and logistical-financial ones, like getting by on limited means, or altering our domestic situation so that we have less upkeep to worry about (mowing lawns, shovelling snow) and more healthcare services at our ready. But later life brings narrative challenges too, in that all of these challenges possess a narrative dimension. In one way or another, they impact the identity-narrative connection that I outlined in Chapter 3. At the risk of portraying them in too-dramatic terms, they can undermine, threaten, or otherwise call into question the stories by which we understand our identity - in short, the stories we *are* (Randall, 2014/1995).

As with the tasks of later life, these challenges can be tightly intertwined, yet each one brings out a slightly different aspect. What is more, each one can contribute to the stress or depression we can succumb to with age - depression that, all too often, is diagnosed as a medical condition and treated with a pill, when a healthy application of narrative care might work just as well. But also, as I'll try to show, each one can be a reality for us at any stage, and not just later life alone. Indeed, they can dog us for decades at a stretch. I would add, too, that these challenges are arguably "spiritual" in nature, insofar as they have to do with how we make meaning amidst our lives.

First of all, there is what my colleague Clive Baldwin, Director of CIRN, has written persuasively about, namely **narrative loss** (Baldwin & Estey, 2015). Narrative loss results when, say, key witnesses to our lives move away or pass away and we're left feeling that no one really knows our story anymore, or worse still, doesn't really care - or at least no one reflects back to us the version of our story with which, for better or worse, we ourselves are most familiar. This sense of loss can hit us when we head off to university, move to a new city, take up a new job, or go through a divorce and have to start all over again. But later life especially renders us susceptible to it. When we retire, for example, or have to "downsize" to different accommodation, such as a nursing home, we have not just fewer things (literally, things) but also fewer rituals and routines to buttress the story by which we've previously defined who we are. Not to mention fewer people, too, some of whom may have known us since we were kids. May Sarton (1981) speaks to the toll this loss, in particular, can take on our narrative identity. Bemoaning at one point how there are "too many deaths to absorb," she observes how "each such death is an earthquake that buries a little more of the past forever" (p. 87).

The term **narrative deprivation**, which Canadian journalist Robert Fulford uses in his book, *The Triumph of Narrative* (Fulford, 1999, p. 201), is linked to narrative loss. A child growing up in a home with few if any books to read, with no adults reading bedtime stories to them, or with lots of yelling and screaming but little by way of conversation stands a good chance, we could say, of being narratively deprived. On a cultural level, however, narrative deprivation has been the lot of indigenous peoples everywhere, given the shameful legacy of residential schools, reservations, and systemic discrimination that has cut them off from their traditional sources of identity, de-storying them on a societal scale.

But it is also how we might describe what happens in some of the environments where we can end up living - like healthcare ones, for instance. Sadly, these can provide us with precious little by way of narrative resources and narrative stimulation. Our stories can be so seldom elicited that they effectively dry up inside us - an extreme form of de-storying that I call **narrative atrophy**. Researchers have calculated, for instance, that residents of many nursing homes can receive as few as six minutes a day of direct contact with fellow human beings. And most of those minutes are taken up, not with conversation per se, but with the sorts of practical tasks around which daily life in such places revolves - getting dressed, eating meals, going to the bathroom, getting ready for bed. I'll come back to this sort of situation next chapter when I talk about narrative environment.

On this point, I'd like to voice a concern that has been brewing away inside of me from my experience as a teacher, seeing far too many of my students sneaking glances at their cellphones during class, whether checking Facebook or sending a text, I don't really know, when I naturally prefer them to remain rivetted to my words. I can't help but wonder whether in a few generations from now, should this trend continue, our capacity to tell stories is in danger of disappearing altogether, and with it our ability as a species to employ narrative thought for making sense of our lives, let alone for being in relationship with others. It would be narrative deprivation writ large.

Narrative knots is a term used by a doctoral student whom I met once at Emory University where I was making a presentation on narrative foreclosure, another challenge that

I'll talk about soon. A licensed therapist in her native Japan, she described the work she sometimes does with clients as a matter of helping them put words onto stories that are all wound up inside of them, of unravelling storylines that are tangled around their hearts and keeping them in a chronic state of **narrative disorientation** - another term that we could use here, too.

I'm a great fan of the murder mysteries of Jonathan Kellerman, particularly those featuring Milo Sturgis, a crusty homicide detective, and psychologist Alex Delaware, his partner in solving crime. But the plots are so intricate and the characters so many that, if I put the book down for more than a few days before picking it back up, I can easily lose the thread. I then have to leaf back through previous chapters, sometimes returning to the beginning altogether, to re-acquaint myself with where the story was headed. But the same can happen with respect to the story of our own life, one that we're squarely in the middle of.

Some years ago, Gary Kenyon and I were telling an older friend of ours over lunch about our (then) new book, *Restorying Our Lives* (Kenyon & Randall, 1997). While we waxed on enthusiastically about how intriguing it was to conceive of our lives in storied terms, the man looked at us askance. "But you can get *lost* in your own story, can't you?," he sighed. The older we get, and the thicker and longer our life story becomes, the more disoriented it is possible we can feel. Midlife in particular can be a narratively disorienting time, as immortalized in Dante's *Inferno*: "In the middle of the journey of our life," the poet writes, "I came to myself within a dark wood where the straight way was lost." But such a sense of lostness - **narrative lostness**, if you like - can prevail on more than the level of the individual alone.

The demise of the sacred masterplots of the world's great spiritual traditions, at least of their ability to claim our unquestioning allegiance, may also be a source of the narrative disorientation that I sense among my students, the majority of them Millenials or Generation Z. I'm alarmed, for example, by the growing number who come to my office each semester and confide in me about the depression and anxiety that they're dealing with in their lives. I can't help but wonder whether this epidemic of angst is tied to the lack of a larger myth that they can situate themselves inside of, one that affords them a sense of purpose and meaning, of being at home in the universe. Rather, as children of a post-modern era, where master narratives of any kind are viewed with suspicion - or at least where, as theologian Thomas Berry (1987) sees it, "we are in-between stories" (p. 187) - they seem so frightfully at sea, overwhelmed with "metaphysical agoraphobia" (Berger, 1963, p. 63) - a case of narrative disorientation and narrative deprivation combined. On this point, it is worth noting, though, that a number of high-scoring participants in our study of resilience told decidedly thin stories about their lives. Yet they went on in some detail about their family, their community, their church, or some grander cause with which they identified or in which they were "embedded" (Furlong et al, 2015). It was as if the strength of their personal story was derived from the strength of that larger story instead.

Sometimes the stories we need to untangle are toxic in nature. They can eat their way into our souls, infecting our self-concept and eroding our sense of self-worth, a condition we could call **narrative contamination**. In his book *The Redemptive Self: Stories Americans Live By*, Dan McAdams (2006) talks, for instance, about "contaminated sequences" versus "redemptive" ones (pp. 213-220). A redemptive sequence is one in which a person had, say, a challenging childhood to start with, yet persevered against all odds, surmounted obstacles of multiple types, and emerged a stronger, wiser person as a result - the sort of rags-to-riches script that fuels the proverbial American Dream. A contaminated sequence works in reverse. The person enjoyed lots of opportunities setting out, but with this, that, and the other, they somehow lost their way and their life went off the rails, almost as if - in their minds at least - their lot in life had been jinxed from the start. Once more, then, it matters immensely how we tell our story.

As their situations become limited due to disability or disease, or any other of the more practical challenges that I listed off above, the narrative to which some older adults end up defaulting leads them to characterize themselves, not as a survivor or an overcomer, but as a failure and a burden. Such a narrative, which New Age author Eckhart Tolle would refer to as a "failed story" (2003), scuttles any efforts they might have made to move forward with their self-esteem intact. It amounts to **narrative unsustainability** (Scheib, 2019, pp. 39-63). Yet again though, I believe, a measure of narrative care could assist them in breaking out of this "vicious cycle" of contaminated storylines (McAdams, 2006, pp. 209-240) and re-storying their lives in more sustainable ways - a theme I'll be returning to in Part Three.

Sometimes, of course, contaminated stories are foisted upon us by others without our consent, albeit with the kindest of intentions. If, for instance, we're experiencing a degree of cognitive impairment and, as the saying goes, have "lost the thread," we may have difficulty telling our stories in ways that others can make much sense of. Accordingly, those others may start silently assuming that, for all intents and purposes, there is no story to tell, and to that extent no self: a condition Clive Baldwin (2006) calls **narrative dispossession**. I'll come back to the topic of dementia in Chapter 8, but in the meantime, any form of prejudice or discrimination is also a means of dispossessing people of their narratives. In effect, we *storyotype* them (Randall, 1995/2014, p. 57), seeing them not as distinctive individuals with stories unique to them alone, but as cardboard caricatures, representatives of some group or race that we happen not to like - which, alas, makes it easier for us to "other" them, to treat them as less than fully human, as "faces without stories" (Gubrium, 1993, pp. 11), if not *de*-story them altogether. Sadly, a more pervasive version of narrative dispossession is at work as well whenever we allow the narrative of decline to plant ageist biases inside of us that taint our treatment of older adults in general.

A variation on narrative disorientation is **narrative incoherence**. Narrative incoherence, simply explained, is being unable to string together a version of events in our life, or of our life overall, that makes much sense, not just to others but to ourselves. Coherence, insists McAdams (2001), is a key criterion of a "good life story" (p. 663). It has to make sense on its own terms. Its elements need to hang together, more or less. They need to co-here. This can't be stressed enough. As the story species, we need things to make some sort of (narrative) sense. In stark terms, the writer Ursula LeGuin (1989) states the issue that's at stake: "An inability to fit events together in an order that at least seems to make sense, to make the narrative connection, is a radical incompetence at being human" (p. 43). Granted, if our lives as texts are, as Mark Freeman puts it, "richly ambiguous" - another term might be "messy" (Denzin, 1997, p. 225) - and if they "cannot ever yield a final closure," then more sense or different sense can always be made of them, and "sense" itself can, of course, take different forms. So, narrative coherence will always be a matter of degree, never once and for all, and take different forms for different folks, depending on their storying style. For some, it may tilt toward the tragic genre, or the ironic or the picaresque, yet possess an integrity of its own that deserves our respect.

That said, what some people can seem to possess is just a smattering of **narrative debris**, a phrase used by our CIRN colleague, John McKendy (2006, p. 473). Before he died back in 2008 (before he was murdered, in fact - which is a whole other story in itself), he was conducting open-ended interviews with male inmates in a maximum security prison. With a number of them, however, due in large measure to the starkly restrictive environment such a setting can be, with its clear (if tacit) limits on who can say what to whom in what ways and when, John found that they had great difficulty marshalling together any sort of a coherent narrative about their lives. It was as if all they had to work with were so many bits and pieces, scraps of memory here and there, with little sense of narrative agency, and even less of "the story of my life" as a whole. Or if they did, then it was one long contaminated sequence. Living in any institution, like a nursing home for instance, a similar difficulty can face us, especially given the six minute limit that I talked about above. As theologian Sam Keen sums the matter up, "you can't tell who you are unless someone is listening" (Keen & Fox, 1974, p. 9).

Narrative disruption (Fireman, McVay, & Flanagan, 2003, p. 9f) occurs when we experience significant change - loss of spouse, mobility, or independence; a diagnosis, a transition, a trauma of any kind - and our working idea of what "our story" is, is temporarily (perhaps permanently) torn asunder. Author Margaret Atwood (1996) gives voice to how this feels in the following passage from her novel, *Alias Grace*: "When you are in the middle of the story it isn't a story at all, but only a confusion; a dark roaring, a blindness, a wreckage of shattered glass and splintered wood; like a house in a whirlwind ... It's only afterward that it becomes anything like a story at all. When you are telling it, to yourself or to someone else" (p. 298). The role of someone else in helping us to experience coherence cannot be stressed too much. How often does it not happen that we go through something huge in our lives - a break-up, a major life change - something that leaves us speechless and bewildered, and we have to ferret out a confidant or friend as quickly as we can, to talk it out, to sort it out? Though the pieces may come tumbling from our lips in no apparent order, with any luck we can be helped to cobble together a version of events that, temporarily at least, enables us to move on.

My friend, Marvin Westwood, is Professor Emeritus of Counselling Psychology at the University of British Columbia. In recent years, Marv has devoted his time to helping veterans of the Canadian military cope with the PTSD that is ripping their lives apart, leading them to domestic stress and broken homes and addictions of one kind or another, even suicidal behavior. The aim of the Veterans Transition Project (VTP) that he and his team have founded is to address the moral injury, and indeed the *soul* injury, that is holding their lives hostage. Through a process called "therapeutic enactment" (Westwood, Keats, & Wilensky, 2003), which combines elements of narrative therapy, psychodrama, guided autobiography, and peer support, Marv and his colleagues work intensely with these men and women, one by one, to go back into the memory of the event that they can't put to rest, can't forgive themselves for, can't form a coherent narrative around. Perhaps it was leaving a buddy to die on the battlefield when the troop was under attack, or mistakenly shooting one of their own soldiers instead of the intended target. Whatever it was, in returning to the original event, surrounded by fellow vets who have revisited similar horrors in similar ways, they are empowered to re-story not just the event in question but, by extension, their life as a whole. Their testimonies to the transformations they experience are inspiring to hear.

My father's mother, or Nana as we called her, suffered a trauma of this type in her late 70s. My father's only sister, our aunt Leah, lived just across the road from her in rural Nova Scotia. Leah would check in on her faithfully every day, and chat with her about all manner of everyday things. They were not just mother and daughter, they were best friends. One morning, while Leah was making her way through thick fog to the local post office where she worked, a truck struck her from behind, killing her at once. In the twinkling of an eye, Nana's world was a wreckage of shattered glass. In fact, she never really recovered, never put the pieces back together. Not long after, Dad invited her to live with us in New Brunswick until things settled down. They never did. Despite the affection that we showed her, she lacked the resilience to re-story, but remained paralysed in her grief. I still recall her sitting with us at suppertime, a sad little smile on her face, or rather, a half-smile, half-grimace. "Nana," one of us would ask in an attempt to cheer her up, "what kind of a day did *you* have?" "Oh, I don't know," she'd answer us back, a distant air about her. "I just sat up in my room and thought about all the *bad* things that have happened to me."

Another term for what Nana was experiencing might be **narrative domination**. This is when our lives are overshadowed by the story of a particular trauma or tragedy, by a particular image of ourselves, or by a particular view of the world overall. "Those who do not have power over the story that dominates their lives, the power to retell it, rethink it, deconstruct it, joke about it, and change it as times change," warns writer Salman Rushdie (1992), pointing out the pathos in this all-too-common situation, "truly are powerless," he says, "because they cannot think new thoughts" (p. 432). Religious or political ideologies come immediately to mind. But so, too, can the narrative of decline that many older adults unwittingly internalize as to what aging itself is about, a narrative that implicitly devalues the worth of our individual narrative. "I'm just an old person," we sigh to ourselves; "there's nothing that interesting about me, really."

Yet another term to use is **narrative imprisonment**. Recalling what I said earlier about obsessive reminiscence, this is when we are stuck inside of, or are holding onto, some story about our life, some image of ourselves, some grievance or regret, some illusion that we insist on clinging to, that we really ought to let go of, but don't know how to, or deep down don't want to, our sense of identity being bound up tightly with it. In his provocative book, *The Truth about Stories: A Native Narrative*, First Nations author Thomas King (2003) shares some of the stories in his own life that, he says, "I have never been able to move past," and that "I will be chained to as long as I live" (p. 9). I'm reminded here also of what William Bridges (1980) says about how a story is "a self-coherent world" with a built-in "immune system" that leads us to resist change (p. 71). This predicament is aptly depicted in this little drawing that I was pulled to the instant I saw it because of the metaphor it affords us for many people's situations, the opposite situation from what Bruner says is preferable as we age, namely "keeping one's options open" and "staying loose ... where one's self-narrative is concerned" (Bruner & Kalmar, 1998, p. 324). The caption I've given it is: *That's my story and I'm stickin' to it!*

A variation on narrative disruption is **narrative disjuncture** (see Randall & McKim, 2008, pp. 192-194) - or, if you like, **narrative dissonance**. With either of these, it's as if we have more than one main storyline about ourselves running side by side within our minds. A haunting book by Lawrence Langer (1991), entitled *Holocaust Testimonies: The Ruins of Memory*, explores the psychic splitting that Holocaust survivors can experience (e.g., the buried self, the divided self, the besieged self, the diminished self). One woman, when asked if she still "lives with Auschwitz," replied matter-of-factly, "No - I live beside it. Auschwitz is there, fixed and unchangeable,"

she explained, "but wrapped in the impervious skin of memory that segregates itself from the present 'me'" (p. 5). In a less dramatic vein, narrative disjuncture is often what leads people to seek therapy.

In their book, *Narrative Means to Therapeutic Ends*, which laid the groundwork for what is known now as narrative therapy, Michael White and David Epston (1990) write, for instance, that: "persons experience problems, for which they frequently seek therapy, when the narratives in which they are 'storying' their experience ... do not sufficiently represent their lived experience ... And," they say, "there will be significant aspects of their lived experience that contradict these dominant narratives" (p. 14). Described in this way, therapy might have been an appropriate intervention for the mother of Canadian memoirist, Sharon Butala (2005).

Butala writes about the narrative disjuncture, and in a sense narrative domination, that she felt her mother was prey to throughout much of her life. "My mother clung to her one story all her life," says Butala, namely that she was "'of good family' ... a family of means ... a family once, long ago, connected to aristocracy" (p. 43f). Her actual circumstances, however, found her in the depths of the Depression, "living in a log house in the northern bush country of Canada, with too many little children, and no money." Her mother's plight, suggests Butala, was that "she saw herself, all her life, as living the wrong life, a tragic life, but which, given her family's ethic, she could not admit to, nor talk about" (p. 44).

Every morning in the coffee shop where I like to write, the same group of older men will shuffle in to shoot the breeze, their banter back and forth orbiting around much the same topics from one day to the next: hunting, hockey, politics, and trucks, or the whereabouts of folks they've known from days gone by (Randall, 2015, pp. 113-116). Often, though, their postures and gestures suggest that, since they've retired, their lives have settled into a resigned mode of existence that smacks of **narrative foreclosure**. Mark Freeman, the scholar who first proposed the term, defines narrative foreclosure as "the premature conviction that one's life story has effectively ended ... that it is simply too late to live meaningfully ... [that] there is little left to do but play out the pre-scripted [tragic] ending" (Freeman, 2000, p. 83). With narrative foreclosure, in other words, our life itself goes on as normal, day in and day out: same old, same old. We go about the business of going about our lives, but in our hearts, our story is all but finished, with small prospect of any new themes, new chapters, new adventures opening up. We live in "epilogue time" (Morson, 1994, p. 193). Here is the rather jaundiced way that the novelist Kurt Vonnegut (1982) puts it: "If a person survives an ordinary span of 60 years or more," he writes, "there is every chance that his or her life as a shapely story has ended and all that remains to be experienced is epilogue" (p. 235).

Narrative foreclosure is itself, of course, a complicated concept, with different sub-types to it, and it can be directed toward the past as much as the future (see Bohlmeijer, Westerhof, Randall, Tromp, & Kenyon, 2011; Freeman, 2011). But my sense is that men are more vulnerable to it than women, in keeping with what I said in Chapter 3 about women having more fluid, more layered, more multi-dimensional storyworlds overall. Certainly, this is the trend that we've been finding in our study of resilience. And older people in general, I would argue, are more likely than the young to succumb to it. That doesn't mean for a minute, though, that the young are immune to it, however temporary their bouts of it may be.

When you're 15, for instance, and your girlfriend or boyfriend brightens up your day by telling you "it's over," it can feel very much like the end of the world. Hurling yourself into the river seems the only reasonable alternative. No matter how vigorously your friends try to assure you that there are many more fish in the sea, or that the one you were so desperately in love with was really not a nice human being, there seems no point in going on. Or, you're in your 30s and your partner walks out, leaving you three children to raise on your own. Or, you're in your 40s or 50s and the company goes bankrupt and you're suddenly out of a job. Or the specialist informs you that your tests have come back positive and that a dark, uncertain future lies ahead. Whatever the scenario, it's not just that one chapter has ended and a new one is about to begin but that the story as a whole feels over. Your life itself keeps rolling along but the story is basically done. So, a state of narrative foreclosure can descend on us at any stage. If I'm honest, this was part of my dilemma during my ministry days. My life was so dominated by the need I felt to be "the minister" that I had given up on being "me." Once more, though, aging itself brings losses and transitions that can set us up for foreclosure in a serious way, a point stressed by Dutch gerontologists, Ernst Bohlmeijer, Gerben Westerhof, and company in their cautious conclusion that it "may have significant consequences for mental health in later life," and may be "a mediating factor between major life-events and depression" (Bohlmeijer et al, 2011, p. 369).

Narrative foreclosure, narrative incoherence, narrative domination - I could continue adding to this list. For example, **narrative diminution** might be another: diminution in terms of the narrowing of the narrative environments we live within, and with them the shrinkage of our storyworlds; diminution from being in relationship with a partner whose version of us is stifling at best; diminution from having too little differentiation in our narrative overall, of having fewer and thinner storylines; diminution from harking bark to the same old limiting memories to buttress our identity or justify our beliefs. But I'll stop for now and state simply that if the tasks of later life were not daunting enough, with the philosophic homework that they represent, then no less daunting are these potential challenges. Herein lies one of the ironies of later life. Just at that stage when this homework is beckoning to us ever more insistently, so too can the obstacles to tackling it pile up in turn, while the energies - physical and psychological - required to surmount said obstacles can seriously begin to ebb.

What does this mean? It means all the more reason why we need others to exercise narrative care with us, which is my focus in Part Three. We need others to foster narrative environments - the topic of Chapter 6 - that will truly be *wisdom* environments, allowing us the special sort of space we need in order to grow into the role of Elder. This sense of older adults as Elders seems to have been lost, however - if it was ever widespread to begin with. Yet interest in Elderhood, including Spiritual Eldering, is happily on the rise - with Schacter-Shalomi's book, *From Ageing to Sageing,* among others, as an example. But the path to Elderhood calls for the company of others, a community of careful, respectful listeners. It's said sometimes in First Nations circles that it takes a whole village to bring up a child. The same is true, I would argue, in aiding older adults to become Elders, to grow old and not merely get old, to keep their stories open, and to share those stories with others who will honour the wisdom that they harbour. I have a few final thoughts, then, before shifting to the topics of narrative environment and narrative care.

NARRATIVE OPENNESS

An assumption running through what I've said so far is that the opposite of narrative foreclosure, as well as many of the other challenges that I've listed, is narrative openness. This is in keeping with what McAdams (2001) has claimed is needed for a good life story. Such a story, he writes, "shows considerable openness to change and tolerance for ambiguity;" and "propels the person into the future by holding open a number of different alternatives for future action and thought" (p. 663). Life stories, he insists, "need to be flexible and resilient" (p. 663). Openness, echoes Betty Friedan (1993) in her inspiring book *The Fountain of Age,* is a "sense that something new can happen," a sense of "age as adventure" (pp. 571-612) - not a tragedy of chronic decline, in other words, but a journey of discovery, the kind that Scott-Maxwell writes about.

Openness sounds fine as a criterion for the middle years of our lives, for the mythic stage. But what about the *post-mythic* stage? Again, how can the older person be expected to keep narratively open when, in reality, their life is drawing to a close? It is certainly a question worth asking. Some would say, for instance, that we are expecting too much of older adults, at least in terms of reviewing, reading, re-genre-ating, and the other sorts of developmental tasks that I talked about in Chapter 4. Theologian, Frits de Lange (2015), has expressed this concern, in fact. In his book *Loving Later Life: An Ethics of Aging,* he points out that "the construction of narrative identity requires an active subject, creating a coherent and enduring 'self' in its imagination." However, some older adults, he points out, particularly those in "deep old age" (p. viii), "may lack the courage and energy to take up that task" (p. 97). They may lack "the narrative capability for identity construction" (p. 98). Rather than pushing them to forge *a good strong story,* writes de Lange, we should help them to develop what he calls "narrative identity, version light" (2011, p. 62).

This is a valid concern, especially for the very frail, for those in deep old age - like my own parents, for instance. Still, the key element for identity construction, I would argue, is not structural openness, as in the events of life continuing to add up. Rather, it is "interpretive openness," the kind of openness that I touched on in Chapter 3 when talking about the parabolic potential of our life narratives. As with novels from which we can derive no end of meaning, interpretive openness has to do, once more, with the quality of our lives as "richly ambiguous texts ... whose readings cannot ever yield a final closure" (Freeman, 1994, p. 184).

In a piece I once wrote entitled "Open stories, open lives: Toward a narrative theology of aging" (Randall, 2014, pp. 353-371), I proposed that a good strong story in later life is characterized by at least four things: (1) openness to ourselves (our past, our future, our unconscious, our dreams); (2) openness to others (including how different others evoke different sides of us); (3) openness to the world (the world of history, of culture, of nature); and (4) openness to stories themselves (including how different stories hold different meanings for us at different times). I'll come back later to what I mean by some of these characteristics, but for now, by way of illustration, I need to say something about an Elder in my own life at present, my good friend, Don.

Don retired from full-time parish ministry some 20 years ago, but that hasn't stopped him from continuing to serve - and to grow. No sign of narrative foreclosure for him. An avid nature-lover, he helps monitor the population of loons in local lakes. A certified spiritual director, he leads individuals and groups of both women and men in exploring their relationship with the Creator, the Mystery, or whatever they are comfortable calling it. And he has a particular passion for the spirituality of men, whom he feels are often developmentally delayed in this regard. This gives him a tremendous sense of purpose and meaning. In fact, I meet with him and four other men for two hours every month in what we call the "Wise Space." Employing a form of contemplative conversation that is modelled on Quaker approaches to spirituality, we share deeply with one another in these sessions about what is happening in our lives. For me, it is a wisdom environment par excellence.

At 85, Don has a cardiac condition that could take him from our midst at any time, and indeed this has nearly happened on more than one occasion in the past few years alone. He is under no illusions about his immortality. Yet neither his health nor his age defines him, nor significantly constrains his activity. He shows up daily at the same coffee shop as I do. He sits in his booth and I sit in mine. He has his pile of books and I have my own. Most of his concern light-hearted topics like ... the history of Christian doctrine, the quest for the historical Jesus, and the links between religion and science. But Don is not just cramming for his finals. He's on a massive adventure. Accordingly, he is keeping himself open - ever curious, ever learning, including learning about himself; always ready to share with others the questions and insights that he's gathering as he goes, so that their lives might be opened out in turn.

For him, the spiritual life is less about the destination than about the journey. He is well educated, to be sure, and has an unusually bookish orientation toward the world. But though his mind is remarkably alert - for anyone, and not just "for someone his age" - it is his attitude toward Life in all of its mystery and complexity that springs to mind when I envision what narrative openness involves.

CHAPTER 6

The Environments In Which We Story Our Lives

Personal stories blend into, are chapters within, community stories.
- David Flynn (1991)

The stories of our culture are those that we hear so often that they cease to seem like stories to us. They are the stories that we take for granted. They are the stories we live by.
- Roger Schank (1990, p. 218)

When I was lad of 11 or 12, a foul-mouthed know-it-all from a grade or two ahead of me told some of us a little poem one day as we huddled around him in the schoolyard during lunch. To me, it sounded terribly funny, something about Mama and Papa doing something while little Jimmy looked on. I didn't really know what it meant, though I suspected it might be a bit on the naughty side. I just liked the amusing way it rhymed. At the dinner table after church that Sunday, I decided to recite it for my sisters and parents, to add a little levity to the occasion. The instant the ditty left my lips, my father put down his knife and fork, scowled fiercely in my direction, and ordered me upstairs. Dinner was officially over. Shortly thereafter, he came up to my room, shut the door solemnly behind him, and proceeded to give me "the talk" - the one about the birds and the bees.

This may be an extreme example, but conversation in the Randall family household, which was also the minister's family household, did not in the least allow that sort of thing to be uttered at the table, or anywhere at all for that matter. In fact, there were quite tight restrictions on what topics could be talked about in what ways, with what words, and when. And there was an implicit code that everyone supposedly respected as to, not just what you talked about, but how you interacted with one another period. Dad, for instance, had more air-time overall, and definitely more authority. What he said was how things were. As the lead character in the Randall family story, his word was law. You never questioned his judgement, or if you did, then you kept your questions to yourself. Any other behaviour was deemed insubordinate and dealt with accordingly.

His hair-trigger temper didn't help the matter either, for you never knew how something you might do or say, or *not* do or say, would set him off with an outburst of anger, a yell or a slap, and then the curtain would drop and black silence would ensue. After a day or more, our dear mother, whose role as "minister's wife" in the family drama, I always figured, was less of a leading one than a supporting one, would urge us to apologize to him, or do whatever was required to get us back into his good graces, even if, as was the case all too often, we had no idea what had set off the storm in the first place. It was not always like this, of course. There were lots of fun family times, and Dad had a silly, playful, loving side that was most endearing - all in all, a good man and a good father. But always in the back of your mind, you remained on your guard, never sure when he would slip into one of his moods and leave you, for no clear reason, feeling at fault.

My own family serving as an example, the term I use for the sort of atmosphere that can prevail within a given family is **narrative environment**. For we don't story our lives in a vacuum, and narratively speaking, none of us is an island. Our storyworlds are never fully our own. They are interwoven in intricate ways with the storyworlds of others, within a complex web of larger settings - larger stories, I sometimes call them - that we're forever moving in and out of, and that themselves are constantly in flux.

NARRATIVE ENVIRONMENT

The concept of narrative environment is one that I find incredibly intriguing. It opens up countless rabbit holes into the complexities of narrative development that there's neither time nor need to go down into here. In his book *Acts of Meaning*, Jerome Bruner (1990) was the first, to my knowledge, to coin the term. In the second part of the book, he reports on a study that he and his colleagues conducted with members of the Goodhertz family. Their analyses of the in-depth interviews carried out with each of them brought out the different versions that each of them entertained of the others, as of the family - and its story - as a whole. As a first foray into what author Arthur Frank (2010) refers to as "socio-narratology" (p. 30), Bruner does a fascinating job of probing the intricate ways in which the narrative environments of families influence the narrative identities of everyone within them, the Randall family being no exception.

I recall occasions when I'd stay overnight at the home of my good chum, Allie Wood, who lived on a farm near the end of the route that the school bus took each day. As we sat around the supper table with his siblings and parents, I felt like I could say almost anything I wanted to (with the exception of what I told at the table that Sunday I just mentioned!), and they would laugh at my silly jokes and find me an amusing, interesting kid. No doubt, they were on their best behaviour, for I was after all the minister's son, and they likely wanted to make a good impression. Nonetheless, I had this feeling that theirs was the sort of free-wheeling, open-hearted household that I would have preferred to be part of myself, not the stifling, egg-shell one that I'd have to return to the following day. How differently would my story have unfolded, I've wondered at times, if I'd gotten my start in that environment instead? It's worth hearing here what psychologist, Sidney Jourard (1971), though somewhat cynical in tone, has to say about things:

> *Day after day for years, family members go to sleep with their family drama patterned in one way, a way that perhaps satisfies none - too close, too distant, boring, suffocating - and on awakening next morning, they reinvent the same roles, the same relationships, the same plot, the same scenery, the same victims* (p. 104).

When asked to explain what I mean by narrative environment, I describe it in a number of ways. First off, I see it as a set of rules or codes, whether explicitly spelled out or (more likely) implicitly assumed, for talking and listening within a given setting. These codes concern everything from use of airtime, to the topics deemed appropriate to talk about (and those that are taboo), to what is funny and what is not - the Randall family environment differing markedly from that of the Wood family in just these sorts of ways.

But the narrative environment of a family also has to do with the actual stories - written or (more likely) oral - that its members refer to, each in their fashion, as emblematic of what the family is about. In the case of my own family, Dad inserted many of these stories (or at least his version of them) into his memoir, *Showers of Blessing*, and then later his book, *Guidelines to Our Ancestors* - subsequently renamed *Guidelines to MY Ancestors*! Of course, the topic of family stories is a whole area of inquiry in itself, with the place and power of the tales that no one ever tells, the skeletons in the closet, as particularly intriguing. In her book, *Black Sheep and Kissing Cousins: How Our Family Stories Shape Us*, sociologist Elizabeth Stone (2004) writes, for instance, about how "people grow up and walk around with [these] stories under their skin" (p. 6f). We tend to "take in these stories without critical analysis," echoes family therapist, Nancy Napier (1993). For this reason, she says, "they live deeply and often unquestioned inside us" (p. 144), which is something Napier suggests can hold us back developmentally. "If we just live old family stories," she suggests, "we may deprive ourselves of the fullness of our capabilities" (p. 146). In *Care of the Soul*, Thomas Moore (1992) sees the influence of family stories in even grander terms: "What the Greek, Christian, Jewish, Islamic, Hindu, and African mythologies are to the society," he says, "stories of the family, good and bad, are to the individual" (p. 29).

Often through the telling and retelling of specific family stories - their signature stories, if you will - the narrative environments of families can serve as the medium for certain formulae for storying our identities as individuals. They can act as conduits for worldviews and values, for convictions, political or religious, about the way things are or the way things ought to be; for broad meta-narratives that we can defer to in composing our personal ones. In that sense, narrative environments come to live within us - not just under our skin but, as it were, in our genes - as much as we live within them.

More specifically, the narrative environments of families provide "narrative templates" or "life-scripts" - what I call "storying styles" and Bruner calls "forms of self-telling" (1987, p. 16) - that we can subscribe to or modify for our personal use. Or that we can rebel against too! Such "ways of telling and the ways of conceptualizing that go with them," says Bruner, stressing how bred-in-the-bone these templates can be, "become so habitual that they finally become recipes for structuring experience itself, for laying down routes into memory, for not only guiding the life narrative up to the present but directing it into the future" (p. 31). And they play a critical role in how we construct our identity in yet another, though related, sense.

Within our unique family drama, our lifestories are inevitably *co-authored* in conjunction with those of others. We are never wholly the authors of our lifestories, in other words, but their co-authors at best. Where my own story ends and that of my sister or mother or father begins is therefore impossible to say, for each of us is effectively a character in the other one's storyworld, and all manner of we-stories end up developing between us. Our narratives are hopelessly enmeshed, and not just in families but in friendships as well. Each friend elicits different sides of us, evokes different versions of our life narratives, and evolves different we-stories with us. From a narrative perspective, then, what Tennyson says is true: "I am a part of all that I have met."

Another point to make is that, in different narrative environments, there are not just different stories swirling in the air, but different sayings in circulation. This becomes particularly obvious when we move from the level of the family to that of a whole region or culture, where different accents, different dialects, and even different languages can be in play. The narrative environment of the Maritime Provinces, a predominantly rural area on Canada's East Coast, where people relate to one another in a generally more playful, laid-back manner, differs noticeably, for instance, from that of downtown Toronto, where downhome Maritime expressions such as *How's she goin', eh?* or *Boys oh boys, she's some nice out there today,* would sound corny and out of place.

Travelling in Norway in recent years, I've had local people say things to me like "we have this expression in Norwegian ...," and then rattle it off to me, followed kindly by the English translation. Whenever this happens, it is clear to me that, although I can make out the meaning of the saying on the surface, I would have to have grown up as a Norwegian myself, immersed in Norwegian language and Norwegian history and the whole Norwegian way of life, to appreciate the range of nuances it possesses, and whatever irony or wisdom it's intended to convey. All of this means that to talk about narrative environment is another way to talk about Culture. Here, environments can vary vastly.

In a book entitled *Narrative and Cultural Humility: Reflections from "The Good Witch" Teaching Psychotherapy in China*, psychologist Ruthellen Josselson (2020) reflects on "the Chinese narrative construction of the world", something she has some appreciation for, given her experience over the past decade of teaching techniques and theories of group therapy to Chinese practitioners. This experience has sensitized her to the multitude of subtle and not-so-subtle ways in which Chinese people differ from people in the West, shaped as they are in a very different social-historical context, with very different forms of self-telling and overarching master narratives informing their lives, and therefore a very different "narrative unconscious" (Freeman, 2002).

Cornell psychologist, Qi Wang (2013), herself a native Chinese person, delves into how the life-scripts or narrative templates that are engrained in Chinese culture, for example, shape the construction of "the autobiographical self" in the deepest possible ways, and thus become, in Bruner's words, "recipes for structuring experience itself" (1987, p. 31). Dan McAdams (2006) sees similar tendencies at work in the American cultural context, arguing in *The Redemptive Self* that "the most powerful life story in America today is the story of redemption" (overleaf). As he explains it, "redemptive life stories reflect and rework such quintessentially American ideas as manifest destiny, the chosen people, and ... freedom" (p. 10f). Clearly, then, the ways in which cultures differ in terms of how people story their lives within them, as well as how their lifestories are enmeshed with those of others, are far too numerous for me to do justice to here.

Still on the enmeshed dimension of narratives, this feature pertains not just to the narrative environments of families and friendships. It pertains to those of marriages, indeed of relationships of any kind, including relationships between clinicians and clients, pastors and parishioners, doctors and patients, spiritual directors and spiritual directees. And it pertains at the level of institutions and organizations; of congregations, communities, and, as we've just seen, entire cultures too. I'll come back in a second to the context of institutions, especially healthcare ones. For now, though, let me underscore the point that narrative environments can be not only macro or micro in nature (from entire cultures to individual friendships), but positive or negative as well.

In other words, the concept of narrative environment is, itself, neutral at base. For particular environments can be either thick and rich or thin and impoverished, six-minute nursing homes as cases in point. They can be fluid or they can be rigid, as in the case of a cult. They can be open or they can be restrictive, like the environment of the average prison, where - as McKendy's research suggests - holding your story together in your heart can be challenging to do. They can be stimulating or stifling, healthy or toxic, and inviting or inhibiting of our narrative development. Put bluntly, they can be *re*-storying or *de*-storying of our souls.

Let me shift, then, to some of the issues at stake in the narrative environments of healthcare settings in particular, settings where many older adults will find themselves living at some point or other and where many of those who provide them with spiritual care can work. To do that, I'll need to say something about narrative medicine.

NARRATIVE MEDICINE

Whatever else it involves, entering a healthcare institution - be it a hospital or a nursing home - represents a change in narrative environment. Depending on our diagnosis or the duration of our stay, it will require us to revise the plot, a little or a lot. To some extent, great or small, it will be a re-storying experience. At best, it's one short chapter in our lifestory overall; other chapters will follow. It's not the *whole* story. At worst, though, it's a de-storying experience. We become "faces without stories" (Gubrium, 1993, p. 11), our identity reduced to a set of symptoms, a diagnosis, a label. Medical staff may be overheard referring to "the gall bladder in 13B" or "the feed in 102." Worse still, we get written off as "a bed blocker" - a horrid term used by the media on occasion to sensationalize the issue of older adults filling up Emergency Rooms due to insufficient resources to keep them in their own homes, or not enough rooms to place them in nursing homes instead.

Put another way, institutionalization in itself can confront us with powerful narrative challenges, for patients and practitioners alike. Those offering spiritual care within such settings - chaplains, social workers, etc. - can feel sometimes like second class professional citizens. As connoisseurs of narrative thought in a context committed to logical thought, they can feel like round pegs in a world of square holes, their work with patients viewed with confusion, even suspicion, by the rest of the healthcare team. For such reasons, and given the emergence of narrative medicine, which I'll turn to in a minute, it might be helpful to re-phrase some of the challenges that I talked about before. Perhaps it could lend added legitimacy to spiritual care if these challenges were cast - tongue-in-cheek, of course - in more medical-sounding terms.

Narrative arrest, for example, would be an acute case of narrative foreclosure. The doctor utters the dreaded word *cancer* and our story stops dead in its tracks. In explaining what he calls "arrested aging," gerontologist Lawrence McCullough (1993), points to a less dramatic form of this condition that aging itself can bring on. "Time," he writes, "has the power to arrest some lives, to bring them to a stop, without death occurring" (p. 185). **Narrative atrophy**, as I hinted before, is our story drying up inside of us because no one ever engages with us anymore, a sad situation that is given poignant expression by Arthur Kleinman (1988), one of the early voices in narrative medicine: "Few of the tragedies at life's end are as rending to the clinician," he writes, "as that of the frail elderly patient who has no one to tell their life story to" (p. 50).

With **narrative anemia**, our stories have become thin, not thick; weak, not strong. Then there is **narrative septicemia**, where the stories we tell about our lives are mostly toxic ones, riddled with contaminated sequences. **Narrative indigestion** is the consequence of undergoing things that we haven't yet been able to put into coherent story form. May Sarton (1980) speaks to this condition when she bemoans in her journal that "the week has been too full. There has been too much experience and too little time to sort it all out, too little time between one thing and another" (p. 178). "I feel cluttered," she says, "by the silt of unexplored experience that literally chokes the mind" (1977, p. 160). Then, alluding to the philosophic homework of later life, she insists: "the deeper the experience, the more time is required to sort it out" (1980, p. 173).

Continuing in this vein, **narrative constipation** would be when we can't get the story out, or don't even know where to begin. Writer Maya Angelou gives voice to the dilemma this involves: "There is no greater agony," she says, "than bearing an untold story inside you." Taking this line of thinking one step further, **narrative compaction** is an extreme form of narrative constipation, in that someone has to *dig* to get our story out, while **narrative diarrhea** would be the opposite condition: the story is flowing but there's little to it by way of substance! Lastly, there is a condition we could call **narrative pregnancy**, which is where there's a new story inside of us just waiting to be born, once the right listener comes along to assist with the delivery. I'll come back to some of these challenges in the following two chapters when discussing how "narrative care" can address them. Before that, though, I want to say more about narrative medicine itself.

Naturally, healthcare settings will each have their own unique story, their own culture, their own narrative environment, some of them quite toxic indeed! But the language and exchanges within them will, understandably, be dominated by a biomedical master narrative, according to which people are spoken of as "patients" first and persons second. Scientific thought will trump narrative thought. And the task-centered nature, the sheer busy-ness, of these environments can easily lead to narrative care being viewed as, basically, a frill. Here is the sort of sign, for instance, that can greet us in doctors' offices nowadays, setting the limits and the tone for the kind of conversation that's condoned:

> *It is now the policy*
> *of this office that we will address*
> *NO MORE THAN TWO*
> *medical concerns*
> *per patient per visit.*

To be fair, those who serve in healthcare settings can be, not just embarrassed by such policies, but profoundly conflicted, given the narrative environment that they have to work within, with its competing pressures to make a healing difference in patients' lives and, at the same time, do more and more with less and less - less time, less money, less personnel. This sort of no-win situation is a recipe for the burnout, if not moral injury, that healthcare staff can often suffer. As Bruce Rybarczyk and Albert Bellg (1997) explain things in their insightful book, *Listening to Life Stories: A New Approach to Stress Intervention in Health Care:* "It's no great secret why we don't listen to patients' stories: we're busy. ... we have information to gather, diagnoses to make, treatment plans to develop, medications to administer, therapy to conduct, and reports to write. But equally," they stress, "we want more than our professional encounter with the patient. We want to connect with patients in a way that feels meaningful - to us and to them" (p. 1).

Here the pioneering work of Rita Charon (2006) needs singling out. A medical doctor herself, with a PhD in English literature to boot, she has led the way in ushering narrative ideas into the medical community. In her masterful book, *Narrative Medicine: Honoring the Stories of Illness*, she offers this definition:

> *Narrative medicine ... understand(s) that patients and caregivers enter whole - with their bodies, lives, families, beliefs, values, histories, hopes for the future - into sickness and healing, and their efforts to get better or to help others get better cannot be fragmented away from the deepest parts of their lives.* (p. 12f)

Charon goes on, using a phrase that appears in the mission statements of healthcare institutions everywhere: "Patient-centred care," she says, "seeks an integrated understanding of the patient's world ... their whole person, emotional needs, and life issues" (p. 27). The "patient's world," I maintain, is their unique *story*-world. Indeed, their stories are central to their identities, their emotions, their beliefs ... and to their physical and mental health. In other words, "patients" understand who they **are** not ultimately in terms of statistics - concerning their white blood count, their body mass index, their glomeruli filtration rate, and the like - but in terms of stories. They understand themselves in terms of *biography*, not biology. In his delightful book, *The Man Who Mistook His Wife for a Hat,* best-selling author Oliver Sacks (1987), a physician himself, says this on the matter: "biologically, physiologically, we are not so different from each other;" however, "historically, as narratives," he maintains,"we are each of us unique" (p. 111) - or as I like to put it, we are each of us *novel*.

Caring for patients' stories, you could say, therefore, is as vital as caring for their bodies. And unhealthy stories, so to speak, may play no less central a role in their overall well-being than unhealthy bodies. In fact, as I've been saying all along, we can sense their stories in their postures and their gestures, their eyes and their sighs. For the stories we are, are always embodied. Therefore, if patients sense that we're less interested in who they <u>are</u> than in what's <u>wrong</u> with them, in what problems they have - physical ones, that is; if we're attentive to their bodies alone and not also to their stories, then in one way or another they may become IM-patient - edgy, depressed, withdrawn, or otherwise non-compliant.

The question for us becomes, then: how can healthcare settings be rendered more re-storying than de-storying? How can we help patients or residents, or indeed older adults in *any* setting, meet the narrative challenges they may face as they age and experience a measure of "narrative repair" (Nelson, 2001)?

The answer in brief, I propose, is **narrative care**, the topic I want to turn to now.

PART III

The Practice of Narrative Care

CHAPTER 7

The Art of Storylistening

A wise old owl sat in an oak.
The more he saw, the less he spoke.
The less he spoke, the more he heard.
Why can't we all be like that bird?
- Traditional

... the crucial thing is the story ... clinical diagnoses are important,
since they give the doctor a certain orientation,
but they do not help the patient.
- Carl Jung (1963, p. 124)

After I left full-time ministry, I had some fairly hefty matters that I needed to sort out. Mostly, they were developmental tasks related to my own story, issues that I'd allowed myself to put on hold during those ten intense years of listening to other people's stories instead, becoming a sponge for them almost. What I was experiencing, as I think back to those days now, was a combination of narrative lostness, narrative disruption, and narrative foreclosure, a condition for which people in ministry, Karen Scheib (2019) proposes, are particularly at risk. What I needed, at bottom, was to find out what "my own story" really was. So I decided to see a counsellor. The decision wasn't one that I made lightly, though. Despite having inflicted on countless parishioners my own seat-of-the pants brand of counselling, there was still this stigma in my head as to what "seeing a counsellor" implied. The experience turned out to be so positive, however, that the stigma soon fell away and I've gone on to see other counsellors since - not so much for Therapy per se but, as I like to think of it, for a periodic tune-up of my emotional well-being. I can't recall the details of what I've talked about with each of these good people - mostly relationship issues, father-son issues, boundary issues, what to do with the rest of my life, that sort of thing. What stands out most for me, however, is the way each of them made me feel.

TELLING OUR STORIES IN WAYS THAT MAKE US STRONGER

The poet Maya Angelou is quoted as saying that "people will forget what you said, people will forget what you did, but people will never forget how you made them feel." I don't really know what therapeutic techniques these counsellors used on me or what school of therapeutic thought they were following. All I know is that I came out of each session feeling better about myself, stronger in myself. Whatever problem I presented with initially didn't magically disappear. It was still there, and I still had changes that I needed to make, homework I needed to do, interpretations of situations I needed to re-assess. But overall I felt affirmed, appreciated, and able to move on. I felt more integrated, more grounded in myself. Not "full of myself," so much as fuller and more authentic inside of myself. I felt like I possessed a unique lifestory that, all things considered, was intriguing and resilient; a story of which I was, in fact, rather proud, and eager to see where it would lead me next.

Barbara Wingard and Jane Lester (2001), narrative therapists who work with Aborigine women in Australia, have written a book whose title alone speaks to what I mean: *Telling Our Stories In Ways That Make Us Stronger*. Telling our stories makes us stronger when we tell them to listeners who listen like the counsellors I've been fortunate to know - insightful listeners, discerning listeners, *strong* listeners. Insofar as there is no story without a listener, insofar as listeners shape what tellers tell, and insofar as in our stories lies our strength, then it all comes down to listening (see Randall, Prior, & Skarborn, 2006). This, to me, is the essence of Narrative Care - listening to people's stories in ways that make them stronger.

Strong listening is the key. But listening in general receives scant attention in our world. As I like to point out, we have tons of Talk Shows nowadays, but few, if any, Listen Shows. In a course I teach each year called Counselling Older Adults, I challenge my students to listen to themselves listening, inasmuch as listening is the heart of all counselling. Between one week and the next, I ask them to notice when and why they listen well and when and why they don't. I ask them to notice how well their friends and family listen to them, and whether they detect any differences in listening styles, in both others and themselves - not *storying* styles but *listening* styles. I even ask them to rate their listening skills on a scale from 1 to 10. Most of them return to class the following week embarrassed at how poorly they find listen to others, not to mention annoyed at how poorly others listen to them, focussed, as those others are, less on what is being said than what they're seeing on the screens of their phones. Be that as it may, I have a few sins of my own to confess.

Some years ago I was chatting with my colleague, Penny Granter, a departmental assistant at our university and someone I love bantering with every time we meet. This particular day she was giving me instructions on how to execute some function on my computer or the photocopier, I can't remember which. As I can often be, with my notoriously short attention span, I kept getting distracted from what she was trying to explain to me and had to ask her to repeat key points. "Bill," she snapped at me, good-naturedly; "do you know what your problem is?!" No, what?, I answered, uncertain what was coming next. "You have a *listening* disability!"

The topic of narrative care is where the rubber meets the road as far as a narrative perspective is concerned. As I've learned from my own intellectual journey, and as the spread of narrative scholarship worldwide is showing, a narrative perspective is totally enticing in itself. For there is no end of questions to be considered, insights to entertain, rabbit holes to scamper down. That said, there is a bottom-line quality and a pragmatic, take-home dimension to this perspective that returns me full circle to my ministerial roots. Listening respectfully and non-judgingly to people's stories - and *for* people's stories, for the stories behind the stories that we hear - tends to change people's lives for the better, because our lives and our stories are effectively one. It's a key way, quite possibly the main way, of "helping" people.

If I can help somebody as I pass along, if I can cheer somebody with a word or song ... then my living will not be in vain - these are lines from one of my father's favourite old hymns. And it expressed a philosophy that he actively practised. I remember the afternoon about ten years ago when I arranged for my mother and him to visit a large local nursing home. In his late 80s at the time, and relying increasingly on a cane to get around, Dad had always been one for planning ahead. "Hope for the best but prepare for the worst" was a cheery little mantra that he often trotted out. At that point the two of them were living quite comfortably in a "senior-friendly" apartment complex, but he could see that this arrangement would not be feasible forever. So I got my friend, Ken, CEO of the nursing home in question, to give us the grand tour, focussing on those sections that had recently been refurbished, all the better to sell my folks on signing up.

Things were proceeding swimmingly, as Ken pointed out the many fine features of his state-of-the-art facility. "Over here is our new dining room, over there a social room to entertain your friends," and so on and so forth. As the four of us inched our way along the corridor, Ken in the lead, father following with his cane, mother lagging behind, sceptical about the prospect of moving at all, we came upon a frail little woman slumped over in her wheelchair, pointed toward the wall, partially blocking our way. Not the sort of scene, I'm quite certain, that Ken would have wanted my parents to witness, nor one that would allay my mother's misgivings. Dad, however, noticing the tag on the back of the woman's chair and familiar with common family names from the surrounding settlements, many of which he had preached in at some point or other, positioned his cane carefully, leaned down and around, and looked her in the eye.

"I see that your name is Mrs Culloden," he ventured, as kindly and clearly as he could, his pastoral instincts thoroughly in gear. "I wonder if you might be from up Williamsburg way?" Slowly, the sat up a little straighter in her chair. "Why, yes, I am!," she answered back in a surprisingly upbeat tone. Their exchange didn't last much longer, and there was no real conversation as such, yet the connection between them, brief though it was, showed me at-a-glance the essence of narrative care. For in less than a minute, Dad had recognized the woman as more than a body slouched in a chair but as a full human being, with a name, a family, a community, and a story - with a bona fide narrative identity, however frayed or forgotten it might have become. And he relayed this recognition back to her. As her brightened demeanour displayed, she could sense it deep inside.

I like to think that that sense remained with her the rest of her day, and that along with her posture, her appetite also picked up; that she ate a better supper, had sweeter interactions with the staff, and enjoyed a sounder sleep that night. I like to think that, roused a little from the narrative foreclosure she may have slidden into, as "the frail elderly patient who has no one to tell their life story to" (Kleinman, 1988, p. 50), she felt reconnected with her life and her self, the flame of her personhood burning a bit brighter in her heart. To me, this little encounter illustrates the essence of narrative care. Indeed, I see narrative care as *core* care, for it goes to the heart - the *coeur,* as the French would say - of who a person is.

In general, narrative care is as much about the attitude that we bring to our interpersonal interactions as it is about any specific activity - though I'll be looking at a range of activities in Chapter 8. And in terms of attitude, narrative care is far more about compassion than pity, empathy than sympathy. The nature of empathy is articulated nicely by homespun poet, Edgar A. Guest (1916, p. 11f), in another little piece that my father liked to quote:

> *When you get to know a fellow, know his joys and know his cares,*
> *When you've come to understand him and the burdens that he bears,*
> *When you've learned the fight he's making and the troubles in his way,*
> *Then you find that he is different than you thought him yesterday.*
> *You find his faults are trivial and there's not so much to blame*
> *In the brother that you jeered at when you only knew his name.*

In the spirit of this poem, narrative care is not about *fixing* people so much as trying to understand them - to *understory* them, if you like. It is about using our innate capacity for narrative imagination to crawl as much as we can inside of their distinctive storyworld. In the same vein, narrative care concerns quality of connection more than quantity of time. In under a minute, my father and Mrs Culloden enjoyed a connection that was healing for them both. Certainly, Dad felt good about himself for treating her with the dignity she deserved, thereby, he hoped, making a modest difference in her situation. Narrative care, if you like, is about fostering narrative environments - however short-lived they may be - that are *wisdom* environments: environments in which people can begin telling thicker, more open stories of their lives, stories that, in the wonderful word used by Arthur Frank (2010), "breathe."

To drill deeper into the specifics of narrative care, which I'm defining here as story*listening*, it is a broad concept that encompasses several forms. It can be long and labour-intensive or, as the saying goes, quick-and-dirty. And it can be practised in, and tailored to, a broad range of contexts, from home care to acute care, from pastoral care to palliative care, from a religious congregation to a community center to a private home. In a healthcare setting, for instance, it can entail attending to a patient's story as much as monitoring their symptoms. "How is your story today?" we're basically asking. It entails remembering that patients are dealing not with medical challenges alone but with narrative ones as well; that their storyworlds are, in some sense, under siege, are "problem-saturated," as narrative therapists would say (White & Epston, 1990, p. 16). Moreover, narrative care can be administered between the lines of other activities (pouring their baths or wheeling them to meals) for, again, it concerns attitude as much as activity, and quality of connection as much as quantity of time. Certainly, it can be informal or formal in nature. It can be practised in the course of ordinary conversation or in full-on psychotherapy.

THERAPY AND STORY

In his extremely valuable book, *Narrative and Psychotherapy*, psychologist John McLeod (1997) insists that "all therapies are narrative therapies" (p. x). In other words, "whatever you are doing, or think you are doing, as therapist or client, can be understood in terms of telling and re-telling stories" (p. x). He goes on: "The importance of listening to *stories*, rather than just employing listening skills in general, is that the story represents the basic means by which people organize and communicate the meaning of events and experiences" (p. x; emphasis McLeod's). McLeod is drawing attention to a highly critical point, namely that in the practice of narrative care, regardless of which therapeutic masterplot we may be working with (from Freudian psychoanalysis to Cognitive-Behavioural Therapy, etc.), the ways we listen to -

and for - a person's narrative is the key.

In his moving and very personal book, *The Call of Stories*, Robert Coles (1989) writes about the two seasoned doctors who were his mentors during his residency in psychiatry at Massachusetts General Hospital. One urged Coles to deploy deductive reasoning as rapidly as possible in order to settle on a diagnosis, however provisional, of the patient's problem, so that treatment could be started straightaway. His other mentor, enamoured of logical thought less than narrative thought, advised Coles to have an actual conversation with the patient, to listen to his or her story, however wild or odd it might sound. "He urged me to be a good listener," Coles writes, "in the special way a story requires: note the manner of presentation; the development of plot, character, the addition of new dramatic sequences; the emphasis accorded to one figure or another in the recital; and the degree of enthusiasm, of coherence, the narrator gives to his or her account" (p. 23). Another of Coles' mentors early in his career was author, William Carlos Williams, himself a physician. Williams went even further in stressing the uniqueness - the novelty - of patients' lives, and thus the importance of listening to their stories. "Their stories, yours, mine," Williams counseled Coles, "it's what we all carry with us on this trip we take, and we owe it to each other to respect our stories and learn from them" (p. 30).

In *On Being a Therapist*, Jeffrey Kottler (2017) devotes an entire chapter to this subject. Its title is: "On Being a Therapeutic Storyteller - and Listener." In it, he agrees with McLeod that "one of the features that unifies all forms of therapy ... is that therapy is essentially a storied experience, one in which the bulk of our time is spent listening to client's reports, prompting them to consider alternative ways to frame those experiences, and then offer other stories in a variety of different forms" (p. 57). He then goes on to list fourteen reasons why "storylistening [is] such a central part of what we [therapists] do" (p. 58f). In a parallel manner, Gary Kenyon and I have included twelve "strategies for storylistening" in our book *Restorying Our Lives* (Kenyon & Randall, 1997, pp. 139-141), a list that I've included in Appendix One.

In his insightful book, *On Becoming A Counsellor*, psychologist-priest, Eugene Kennedy (1972), includes a chapter entitled "Listening to the Story." In it, he advises story-listeners to be attentive to "the feeling tone" that a client uses in telling their story (p. 106) - what McAdams would call their narrative tone. He urges us to note the perspective in time from which they tell it (is it oriented primarily toward the past, the present, the future?); and to their "central identification" (p. 106), which is to say whether they characterize themselves passively or actively within it, as victim or as agent. Critical to attend to as well, says Kennedy, is obviously "the theme" (p. 107) - something he reminds us "is central to any narrative" and is "the thread of meaning" that ties together many of the specific stories that a client might tell. Overall, he warns counsellors against getting caught up with the details on the surface of the client's story, but instead to "hear *into* the narrative" (p. 108). In the process, maybe, we can catch wind of the real story, the deeper story, that the client is attempting to tell. In the words of fellow counsellor, Charles Winquist (1980), "we tell a story in order to find a story" (p. 43).

What I hope is becoming clear from all of this is the value of narrative care in working with anyone, to be sure, but especially perhaps with those in the narrative phase of their lives, the post-mythic phase. In other words, those whose main means of making meaning, of seeking coherence and healing, is through telling and retelling the *stories* of their lives. But what in particular might we focus on in practising narrative care with older adults? This is the more practical kind of question that I want to turn to next.

CHAPTER 8

The Craft of Storylistening

*Listening to another's life story means
being a witness to what they are saying.
It means really caring about what they have to tell you.*
- Robert Atkinson (1995, p. 123)

There is no story without a listener.
- Susan Baur (1994, p. 29)

Narrative care is, at base, an art. Yet it clearly has a craft dimension, for any number of strategies can be enlisted to practice it effectively, whether with older adults or with anyone of any age, and whatever the context - a hospital, a palliative care unit, a retirement home, a nursing home, a congregation, a counselling office, or a person's private abode. It's the craft side of narrative care which - admittedly, quite briefly - I'll be sketching out here.

THINGS TO WATCH FOR AND LISTEN FOR IN PRACTISING NARRATIVE CARE

For starters, there are certain things that we can *watch* for as clues to an older adult's storyworld, to their distinctive storying style, to the narrative environments in which they have been shaped and the narrative tasks and challenges that they face. These include the kind of music that they like, the people who visit them, the magazines they read, the hobbies that engage them, and the movies they enjoy, not to mention the photos or mementoes that surround them. For these sorts of "cherished objects" (Sherman, 1991) can be the symbol or the trigger for all manner of stories lying underneath; the tip of the narrative iceberg, if you like (see, e.g., Randall & Robinson, in prepartion). Then there are the sorts of books that are sitting on their shelves, especially if one of them is a memoir they've written themselves! Above all, there are the lines on their faces and the looks in their eyes, and the stories these bespeak. But, for certain, there are things to *listen* for as well.

Among the many things to listen for, to be attentive to, are the narrative tone with which a person tends to talk, and the types of reminiscence in which they appear to engage. Is it mainly obsessive or escapist, for example, or does it lean toward the integrative type? Then there is the way that they characterize themselves amid their life's events, plus the telltale phrases they may use and the themes that these betray. Let me give an example.

Years ago, I was teaching a course entitled *Narrative Knowing and Learning* for graduate students in adult education. One of the exercises I had them do was to break into groups of three and share with each other the story of their life, one at a time, in whatever way they chose to tell it, while the other two listened and took note. As it happened, one of the students had once taught me English in high school, a woman for whom I held fond memories because of the high marks that she gave me on my essays and how she therefore helped me to believe that I might have a glimmer of intelligence after all. Now in her early 60s, she was finally pursuing her Master's degree. Since there wasn't an even number of students for the class to divide up into threes, I joined the group that she was in. As my mother would say, the woman had had "a hard life," which came through clearly in the narrative tone, the feeling tone, with which she told her story. Though she had had a full life as well, with much in it of which to be quite proud, the way that she narrated it conveyed something different.

As she listed off the many things that she had done - come through a divorce, raise three children on her own, survive cancer, and now be getting another degree - she kept using the phrase "somehow I managed to ..." (come through a divorce, raise three children, etc.). But she said what she said with a sad sort of sigh that suggested to the two of us listening that she didn't quite believe herself; that she had accomplished lots, to be sure, yet somehow wasn't supposed to. It was as if she weren't really the center of her own story but rather a victim of circumstances, looking on from the sidelines, whose narrative agency was continually in question; or if not a victim, then a tragic hero at best, with emphasis on the tragic more than the heroic.

Along with these sorts of telltale phrases, it's important to listen for the conflicts and tensions that run though a person's self-storying; to be alert to the "nuclear episodes" (McAdams, 1996, p. 140) or "signature stories" (Kenyon & Randall, 1997, pp. 46-49) around which their sense of self revolves. Then there are the sorts of family stories that they may tell, the themes that run through these in turn, and the window they provide onto the type of family drama, the narrative environment, in which they've been brought up; to say nothing of the larger stories - of community, cosmos, or creed - with which they identify or to which they allude.

Overall, it is critical to listen not just to what they tell but what they withhold. For instance, are there "shadow stories" (deMedeiros & Rubinstein, 2015) that lurk between the lines - for example, stories about a painful first marriage, or a life-altering trauma, that is otherwise glossed over? Are hints dropped about possible selves and unlived lives that they harbour within them? Are there stories that they don't maybe know how to tell at all, risky stories that they've never felt safe enough to share - the kind that they might preface with a comment like: "I've never told this to anyone before, but ...."? Then there are the "preferred narratives" (Freedman & Combs,

1996) that they would like to tell, and to live. There are, for instance, "stories of strength and meaning," to quote SuEllen Hamkins (2014) in her book *The Art of Narrative Psychiatry*. By this she means "stories that are implicit in the patient's presenting narrative, but that may have been unrecognized and, as yet, untold" (p. xxii). There are also the "counter-stories" (Nelson, 2001) that are coursing through them, like cross-currents in a stream - like the hero version in my teacher's story that ran counter to the tragic version to which, it seemed, she had defaulted. And then there are the "sacred tales" (Ruffing, 2011) that have been awaiting the right time and the right listener to lure them to the surface. Hopefully, when the teller is ready, the listener will appear.

AVENUES OF ENTRY INTO PEOPLE'S STORYWORLDS

Narrative care with older adults is scarcely rocket science, in the sense that several sorts of - often quite ordinary - activities can stimulate the storying process, and as a result, can re-start life narratives that are possibly stalled. I think of these activities as avenues of entry into the multi-layered realm of another person's storyworld, a world, it needs remembering, that is deeply unique, or as I like to say, *novel*. Among such activities, at a very basic level, can be a window box or a shadowbox outside of a nursing home room. Stocked with memorabilia from a resident's life (photographs, diplomas, medals, a cherished object or two), such things can provide visitors to that resident a quick glimpse into the key people and accomplishments in his or her life, perhaps prompting a question with which a healing conversation could begin.

Any mode of creative activity can also open avenues into memory and thus increase occasions for storytelling and storylistening. Indeed, encounters with creative works of any sort can spark narrative activity and narrative reflection. An intervention developed by Dutch gerontologists called "creative reminiscence," for instance, uses painting, collaging, and poetry writing to invite older adults in the grips of depression to generate metaphors that point to themes in their life stories that might otherwise go unacknowledged (Bohlmeijer, Valenkamp, Westerhof, Smit, & Cuijpers, 2005). The same gerontologists have developed a program for life review therapy with older adults called "Finding Meaning in Life" (Bohlmeijer & Westerhof, 2011), which has been shown to lower their depressive symptoms immediately following the intervention and even six months further on (Bohlmeijer, Kramer, Smit, Onrust, & Marwijk, 2009).

By the same token, the power of popular past-times like scrapbooking and family genealogy to prompt narrative reflection on the different dimensions of one's story must not go unnoticed. So, too, must making lists. Lisa Nola (2007), for instance, has published a book entitled *Listography: Your Life in Lists*, each page of which is otherwise blank yet is headed by instructions like: "List your guilty pleasures," "list your favourite songs," "list your biggest acts of kindness" - a great way to prime the memory pump and prompt awareness of how varied and interesting your life has actually been. From my own research with older adults, however, I've found that many of them have so deeply internalized the narrative of decline that they seriously devalue their own uniqueness and worth. When asked to talk about their lives, they start off with some dismissive comment like "there's not much to tell, really. My life has been pretty normal, nothing terribly interesting about it at all." The simple act of making lists could unseat such a sad self-assessment and get the narrative juices flowing yet again.

As I alluded back in Chapter 4, a program entitled *Celebrating Our Stories* has been implemented at the nursing home where my parents were given their grand tour. In it, with the aid of a list of leading questions (Sanders, 2007), selected residents are interviewed at length concerning the different aspects of their lives: their childhood, their jobs, their hobbies, their relationships, and the like (Noonan, 2011). Their answers are then assembled into a book that is presented to them at a public ceremony attended by family members, fellow residents, and friends from the community, plus staff and administration from the nursing home itself. The centrepiece of this ceremony is a 15 to 20 minute video featuring photos from various chapters of that resident's life, samples of their favourite music, and statements that they made during the interviews themselves that afford viewers a little window onto the full sweep of their world. Having attended several of these ceremonies I can attest that there is seldom a dry eye in the crowd. The impact of this program on the narrative environment of the institution as a whole has been, as the phrase goes, culture-changing. In making all parties that much more mindful of how *every* resident has a story, that they are a full human being no matter the limitations that they're experiencing now, it has enhanced the quality of care that *all* residents receive (see also Villar & Serrat, 2017; Berendonk, Blix, Randall, Baldwin, & Caine, 2017).

An approach to memoir-writing pioneered by veteran gerontologist, Jim Birren, called "guided autobiography" invites people to delve into their life stories one theme at a time in the camaraderie of a group (Birren & Cochrane, 2001). Life-writing groups structured along similar lines, such as those that gerontologist Kate de Medeiros (2011) has studied, or even simple "storytelling circles" (Pohlman, 2003) - in which story cards, photographs, random objects, or other quite ordinary cues are used to stimulate recollections - these can have a similarly therapeutic impact in terms of helping older people address issues of narrative foreclosure, narrative deprivation, and the like. Though practised more commonly with younger age groups, narrative therapy per se is increasingly employed with older clients too (Osis & Stout, 2001). In one case, an 80-year old widow wrestling with depression was encouraged to critique the master narrative of aging as decline that had usurped her self-image. In reaction to this negative larger story, she began revising her life narrative and re-casting herself amid it from a "failure" to a "survivor" (Kropf & Tandy, 1998).

To address **narrative loneliness** especially, Danish psychologists Morten Hedelund and Andreas Nikolajsen (2013, p. 1) have devised an innovative intervention called "Telling Stories for Life" that combines life story interviewing strategies with the intensive questioning typical of narrative therapy. In a small group setting with coffee and cake around the kitchen table, the aim is to engage older adults from the neighbourhood who have been identified as being at-risk for depression due to social isolation. The result is often the formation of fresh friendships and a heightened sense of narrative agency - of narrative interesting-ness, if you like - for each of them. Once again, I would argue that what such persons may need most of all is not more medication so much as a liberal dose of narrative care.

Along similar lines, my friend Richard Lafleur, a professor of psychology at West Georgia State University and director of pastoral counselling for a huge congregation in suburban Atlanta, has set up a program aimed at Vietnam veterans so that they can tell their often tortured, troubled tales in a safe, respectful space. Each person gets to take the talking stick or the talking stone and hold forth for as long as they need to on whatever is weighing on their heart. A less intensive intervention than what Marv Westwood has pioneered, it is effective nonetheless in providing veterans with the very sort of healing environment that is otherwise missing from their lives. The name of the program is "Just Listening."

One activity that should never be discounted as a mode of narrative care is simple conversation. In the retirement home where my mother resides, there is this one woman whom we chat with often during the many laps around the premises that my mother makes with her walker to keep herself in shape. Though needing a walker herself, plus dealing with a significant loss of vision, the woman is well-educated, has a busy career behind her, and exhibits no signs of dementia whatever. Because she finds it challenging to read, however, she passes her time sitting in a corner of the social room doing jigsaw puzzles by herself. For she finds the various activities that the staff of the facility offer every day to be not just unstimulating but juvenile almost, tailored as they are to the majority of residents who are in some stage or other of cognitive decline. In a word, the woman is bored. And if her boredom is not soon addressed, I'm afraid, it's in danger of deteriorating into a case of narrative atrophy! What she wants most, I've sensed from our visits, is an invigorating exchange with anyone, young or old, on any topic that taps into her store of interests and experiences, memories and stories. So then, plain old ordinary conversation as a form of narrative care - this, too, needs adding to the list.

THE BENEFITS OF STORYLISTENING

As these different examples attest (and many more could be included), affording older adults occasions to recount and reflect on the stories of their lives has benefits that are, broadly speaking, *therapeutic* in terms of enhancing their mental, emotional, and even physical well-being. Among these benefits are an increased sense of agency, purpose, and meaning, while at the same time, a decrease in anxiety, depression, and stress, one consequence being, so some research suggests, a strengthened immune system overall (Pennebaker & Seagal, 1999). In a naturally cathartic manner, people can experience the resolution of past grudges or regrets; the assimilation of negative events into their sense of self; and the satisfaction of passing along to others their unique life lessons, or their "ordinary wisdom" (Randall & Kenyon, 2001), thus strengthening their sense of legacy and generativity. Involved as well can be the realization, sometimes liberating, often surprising, that their life has not been what they thought it was, that a measure of *re-genre-ation* is possible, in fact. As Harry Berman (1994) puts it, perhaps they thought their life was "almost over," but instead, "it turned out there was a lot more to it" (p. 180).

Another very practical benefit of narrative care in a healthcare context is in building a trusting rapport with an older patient. A nurse approached me one time after I had spoken on these themes at an eldercare conference on Prince Edward Island. "Thank you for what you said about the importance of listening to older people's stories," she said, "because my co-workers often criticize me for 'spending too much time' with the patients. It's like they see it as a frill somehow, as 'soft' nursing rather than the real thing. The way I look at it, though," she explained, "is that getting to know them as individuals ends up saving us time in the long run. Because we'll have more of a relationship with them, and that relationship will make it easier to carry out all the other tasks we have to do with them. More than this, though, I find them each so interesting! I learn so much from them, and from their stories. It makes my work that much more meaningful for *me*!"

NARRATIVE CARE FOR THOSE WITH DEMENTIA

I've already hinted at the implications of a narrative perspective for practice with older adults who are wrestling with depression. Among these are the possibility that their depression is due, in part at least, to being overwhelmed by the narrative challenges facing them in later life, that they are stuck within the constrictive environments of families, relationships, or institutions, that they are caught in a crisis of meaning - from which the chance to reflect on the stories of their life could help to set them free.

The topic of depression and narrative deserves a whole chapter in itself, without a doubt, as does that of dementia and narrative. Still, there are at least a few implications of a narrative perspective for those living with this condition that I can point to briefly here. Key among these, I believe, would be that being unable to narrate their lives in ways that make much sense to others doesn't mean that there is no story, and thus no person, present. Here Clive Baldwin's work bears mentioning again.

Insofar as our individual stories are co-narrated and co-authored in relationship with others amid a network of larger stories in turn, so too, he says, are our assumptions about "story" itself, and thus what constitutes a "good" or "normal" *life* story. For Baldwin, who also stresses the need of a "narrative ethics for narrative care" (2015), this insight should inform our every interaction with those living with dementia. The problem behind the narrative dispossession to which we might otherwise subject them, he argues, lies less with their inability to string together a story that is coherent to us than it does with our overly linear, Western assumptions as to what constitutes "narrative coherence" in the first place (Baldwin, 2006). According to those assumptions, in order for something to be a bona fide story, it has to have a beginning, middle, and end, and in that same order. A kind of "narrative quilting" (p. 106) could be at work instead, however; namely a patchwork mode of storytelling through which identity-work is nonetheless occurring, with the thread of the plot, so to speak, still discernible, albeit in a less obvious, more metaphorical manner.

This is a similar point to what nursing professor, Jane Crisp (1995), proposes, based upon her experience of caring for her aging mother. The more Crisp thought about them, the more her mother's chopped-up confabulations seemed to take the form of "waking dreams," replete with allusions to recurring themes in the woman's life across the years. If not the vehicle of "historical truth" concerning that life, they felt like to Crisp like windows into "narrative truth" (see Spence, 1982).

Among the many programs that have been implemented to spark narrative activity among persons with dementia, innovations such as *True Doors* (van Diepen, 2014), *Music and Memory* (Cohen, 2010), and *TimeSlips* (Basting, 2003) have proven especially effective as avenues of entry into their storyworlds, as foreign as those worlds can at first feel to us. As philosopher Hilde Lindeman (cited in de Lange, 2015) would say, they are ways of "holding someone in personhood" (p. 134). As such, they are expressions of "preservative care" (p. 135f). If none of us is ever, strictly speaking, the authors of our own lifestories but always - with others, within various narrative environments - their co-authors at best, then the role that we play in preserving the personhood of persons with dementia is, indeed, best captured by terms like "storykeepers" or "storycatchers" (Baldwin, 2005). This insight, in addition, harmonizes with a view that I've put forward elsewhere (Randall, 2010b) that the line between "normal" autobiographical memory and the memory of someone with dementia is anything but precise, certainly less precise than we otherwise assume. For many of the memories around which we construct our sense of self, upon honest inspection, are in one way or other concocted, blurred, or tangled. They are "entangled," as dementia scholar Lars-Christer Hydén (2017) expresses it, with the storyworlds of many others in our lives - parents, siblings, partners, friends. And, they are ultimately not factual at base but factional at best. Once more, for all of us, memory is mostly a matter of faction.

NARRATIVE CARE FOR THE DYING

Finally, a narrative perspective has implications for practice with those nearing death. And though this topic, too, merits a chapter of its own, a few of these can be noted here.

For one thing, the need typically intensifies within us to get "ready to go," to quote Mr Cain. Wrapped up in this is the need to pull together the threads of our life, to tie up loose ends, to mend fences and make amends wherever possible, and to deal with any outstanding developmental business, as per the many R's that I talked about in Chapter 4. Overall, the need intensifies to arrive at some sense of narrative cohesion concerning our life by engaging in a measure of life review (see Kuhl, 2002). To put this another way, as with any story, "the sense of an ending" (Kermode, 1966) grows that much more immediate, and as such can be an incredible motivator. If, as claimed by those who report having had Near Death Experiences (see Long & Perry, 2016, p. 19f), the first stage of existence beyond this one is taken up with a thorough review of the life that we've just lived, then this intensification is perhaps not so odd - a way of getting a head start on a process that we'll have to go through anyway! With the need to review their life, though, is the need to identify their unique store of wisdom, of life lessons, of stories for those they leave behind; their narrative legacy, in other words.

Also, as opposed to *fore*-closure per se, they may crave a healthy measure of closure instead; the feeling, in other words, that the life that they've lived, all things considered, has had meaning and merit. Due in part to a decline in sheer physical energy, they may have a preference less for full-on life review, or for "big story narrative reflection" (Spector-Mersel, 2016), than for recounting smaller stories instead, ones that encapsulate the best, the most meaningful, or the most sacred parts of their lives across the years. In analysing interviews with dying patients whom he has worked with in storytelling groups, Norwegian gerontologist Oddgeir Synnes (2015), for instance, has identified a species of escapist reminiscence that he calls "nostalgic stories." By this, he means small stories about pleasant times or poignant times that gently rekindle the person's sense of narrative identity - albeit "version light" (de

Lange, 2015, p. 100) - in the face of their impending demise: stories of happy family picnics in the fields above the fjörd when they were a little girl, that sort of thing.

Lastly, the dying person may be open to what be could be called **narrative disengagement**, which is to say, to transcending their life story (Randall, 2009). To reword slightly the question that Scott-Maxwell (1968) has put to us: "when at last [death] has assembled [our life] together, will it not be easy to let it all go, lived, balanced, over?" (p. 40). The dying individual may be open, as well, to entertaining more positive storyings of Death itself. Not as The End in any ultimate sense, in other words, but rather as what literary scholar, J. Hillis Miller (1978), commenting on the parallels between death and endings in fiction, calls "the most open-ended ending of all" (p. 6). Not as a termination, we could say, but as a transition ... to The Next Chapter, to The Other Side, to The Big Adventure. They may be open to approaching death not with dread, in the final analysis, but with wonder, seeing it as less an ending than a beginning - a birth.

NARRATIVE CARE IN A NUTSHELL

By way of wrapping up, narrative care involves listening to people's stories in such a way that we foster an inviting narrative environment - a *wisdom* environment - where they can cope with whatever narrative challenges they may face in their lives: narrative foreclosure, narrative diminution, narrative loss, and so forth. It involves fostering a space where they can cultivate a stronger story of their lives, in the process enriching their inner resources and feeling fuller in themselves, and with that feeling becoming more resilient overall. It involves fostering a space where they can air long-buried stories, stories they haven't known how to tell at all. It involves fostering a space where they can not just *tell* their stories but can listen to what their stories tell them, where they can *read* their stories too. It involves assisting people to expand, and be expanded by, their stories. It involves aiding them in addressing the philosophic homework of later life, in keeping their stories open, in helping them to experience their own aging as a matter, not just of getting old, not just of "withering", as May Sarton says, but of *growing* old. To borrow once more from Beuchner, it involves supporting people as they seek to "read with open minds the story [their] life is writing, and learn."

Narrative care involves helping people to appreciate the parabolic potential of their stories; helping them to catch sight of the Truth that lies within them, something Scott-Maxwell says "a long life" can make us feel closer to. What dying people in particular want, says David Kuhl (2002), a palliative care physician who interviewed dying patients for his PhD in counselling psychology, is not platitudes, not false encouragement, but truth - from others and from themselves - "the truth of who you are" (p. 179). And truth, he adds, "has to do with telling your personal story" (p. 171). "In your own life story," echoes Robert Atkinson (1995) in his lovely book, *The Gift of Stories*, "is where you will find *your* truth" (p. 43; emphasis Atkinson's). Narrative care involves fostering a space where people can see their own stories as entry-points - not as obstacles but as entry-points - into the Divine; a *sacred* space, if you will, where their sacred tale can gain, at last, a proper hearing.

Narrative care, ultimately, means overcoming whatever listening disability we may have and becoming deeper listeners to people's stories, for deep listening elicits deep telling. It means being agents of re-storying and not de-storying in their lives. It means being storykeepers, holding their secrets safe in our hearts, honouring the wisdom that their story bears. It means being story catchers. "Storycatchers," writes Christina Baldwin (2005), "come whenever we are in crisis to remind us who we are. Storycatchers," she says, "entice our best tales out of us: they turn with a leading question, a waiting ear, and their full attention" (p. xiv). It means being "story companions to one another," to borrow from pastoral theologian, Karen Schieb (2016); in other words, "listening in the midst of suffering, listening as a life unfolds, listening for the presence of God" (p. 61). As expressed by Janet Ruffing (2003), a leader in the field of narrative and spiritual direction, it means "the art of listening sacred stories into speech" (p. 38).

Once more, then, narrative care with older adults is not rocket science. I don't mean by this for one moment that it is simple or unsophisticated. Far from it. For it involves much by way of imagination and intuition, of subtlety and vulnerability, plus an intricate set of skills, often hard-won, for burrowing into another human being's storyworld. That said, compared with most tests and medications, it is not wildly expensive. It is low cost and low tech. But, it is high impact. A little bit goes a long way. And it is potentially transformative in nature, for teller and listener alike, for it is ultimately a relationship, not a task; not just one more thing to be added to our list. It is a relationship where we may become characters in, even co-authors of, a key chapter in the evolving narrative of a person's life. As such, narrative care is implicitly therapeutic in nature (Gardner, 1997). If you will, it is thera*poetic*. And compared to other modes of care - nutritional care, pharmaceutical care, and the like - it is every bit as vital. What many people may need most, I will say yet again, is not one more medication but, instead, a healthy dose of narrative care. Narrative care is emotional care, spiritual care, and patient-centered care wrapped up in one, for it lies at the center of each. It is core care, for it goes to the heart - the cœur - of who a person is. And it is what, without having a name for it, draws many of us to the helping professions in the first place. Lastly, though, narrative care begins at home ... which leads me to the topic of <u>self</u>-care.

CHAPTER 9

Taking Narrative Care of Ourselves

Healers are hosts who patiently and carefully listen to the story of the suffering strangers. ... As healers we have to receive the story ... with a compassionate heart, a heart that does not judge or condemn but recognizes how the stranger's story connects with our own.
- Henri Nouwen (1976, p. 89f)

We learn who we are through the stories we embrace as our own.
- Sallie TeSelle (1975b, p. 160)

Narrative care has a craft dimension, to be sure. But it is ultimately not a technique so much as an art, one that some wield more naturally than others. Whether it comes naturally or not, however, the heart of this art is self-awareness, awareness of ourselves. By this, I mean awareness of our own unique story, since our "self" and our "story," as I've been stressing from the start, are effectively one. As ethicist Stanley Hauerwas (1977) expresses it, "the mysterious thing we call a self is best understood exactly as a story" (p. 78). But let me take this one step further.

In the chapter on spirituality as a narrative endeavour, I suggested that we have faith, that we believe, that we have spiritual experiences, not despite our own stories but through them. In the same way, we listen to the stories of others not in some bias-free, story-neutral space but - try as we might to avoid doing so - *through* our own stories. Instead of seeing this as a failing, though, we should see it as an advantage, for in our stories lies our strength. We can have all the training we like in counselling strategies and therapeutic steps, but when it comes to listening deeply and respectfully to a fellow human being, our own life stories are often our greatest resource. A particular conversation comes to mind as impressing this point upon me.

As I've mentioned different times already, not long after leaving full-time ministry, I embarked on an intensive intellectual-emotional journey that eventually led to completing my doctorate. My main mentor during that three-year period was Don Brundage, Professor of Adult Education at the University of Toronto and a pioneer in the field of adult learning, a man who confided to me once, in fact, that he would have preferred to be a minister instead - just the opposite of me. I couldn't have asked for a more supportive presence during those endless days of working on my dissertation.

Early in that process, I recall sitting in his office high above Bloor Street overlooking the university football field, bemoaning the fact that, at 39, I was somewhat late to be starting doctoral studies. I wished aloud to him that I could go back and do things differently, not spend all those years in ministry. Compared to the glitz and glory that I fancied an academic career would bring, they seemed something of a needless detour. Kindly but curtly, Don cut me off. "Bill," he said to me with passion, "those years of ministry you've had are pure gold - all those people you dealt with, talked with, listened to. Think of how much you've learned from them about human nature, about the human condition. Why, your colleagues in this program would give their eye teeth to have the wealth of experience under their belts that you have under yours!"

THE MYSTERY IN MY STORY

When I ended the last chapter by saying that narrative care begins at home, I meant that taking narrative of others - older adults in particular, given that they are in the narrative phase par excellence - is dependent on our taking narrative care of ourselves. Appreciating how interesting other peoples' stories are - not storyotyping them, in other words, not de-storying them in any way - is linked to honouring how interesting our own stories are as well, no matter our age. One time, years ago, in my course on Narrative Gerontology, the class was discussing what it was like to engage in the various reflective exercises that I had them do to get in touch with their own unique life-narratives. One student's comment still stands out. Because of all these activities, she said, she was starting to appreciate "the mystery in my story."

Awareness of our own stories, in all their mystery, is essential for helping others. We can't offer ourselves as agents of re-storying in their life-narratives if we are oblivious to the dynamic dimensions of our own, how our own past, too, is always changing, never static. We can't be a discerning story catcher or a compassionate story companion if we're unmindful of our own unique storying style, let alone the complexity of narratives in general; if we lack **narrative literacy**, so to speak. By narrative literacy is meant a basic understanding of what stories are and how stories work - life stories, in particular. In all, to the degree that listeners shape what tellers tell, then listening deeply to another person's lifestory hinges on our capacity to listen deeply to our own. But what does this mean? What does narrative self-care involve?

It involves, first of all, honouring our own stories as our greatest resource in listening to those of others. Within this, it involves acknowledging the narrative tasks and narrative challenges that face us in our own developmental journey. It involves identifying and, as much as possible, integrating the troubles and traumas, the possible selves and the unlived lives, that make our own story itself so intricate and multi-layered. It involves being mindful of the philosophic homework that lies before us so that we, too, can be growing old and not merely getting old. It involves not just telling our stories, but listening to what our stories tell us. It involves harvesting the meanings they contain; discerning the parabolic potential in the texts of our own lives too. Through one form or another of autobiographical learning - of *storywork*, as I like to call it (Randall, 2010) - it involves keeping those texts open and evolving, resilient and strong.

On a practical level, narrative self-care can involve making an inventory of the various things that we've done or said, experienced or seen, that could serve as entry-points into other people's storyworlds. For instance, it can involve making lists (Nola, 2007). I've had the good fortune to travel a fair bit, both as a student and especially as a professor. In listing off the various adventures that I've had, I can see how each of them provides me with potential points of contact with someone else's life. Perhaps I've visited the culture, the country, or the city where they hail from initially? If so, then I can imagine a little what their life was like growing up, why they think and are the way they think and are, how in general they story their lives and their world.

I've also been curious all my life about geography. I love nothing better than poring over maps. For this reason, I was rather bad, I believe, at conducting research. Interviewing older adults in the qualitative component of a longitudinal study of people 80 and over that I was directing a decade or so ago, I could easily get sidetracked from the main aim of the interview if the participant happened to mention the village where they grew up. All too frequently, I would cut them off in the middle of their narration to ask where exactly that was. In turn, this might lead to us learning that we knew certain people in common and thus take us off-track all the more (Randall, Prior, & Skarborn, 2006). The same tendency that compromised the detached, objective stance of a researcher, however, worked to my advantage when I was a minister. For my innate curiosity about not just geography but history and nature afforded me an array of ways to crawl inside of a parishioner's world, to build bridges of imagination into what their lives were like.

The key here is *narrative* imagination (Andrews, 2014). This makes reading stories of any kind - short stories, novels, biographies, autobiographies - absolutely critical, not just to expanding our personal storyworlds but to expanding our appreciation for the ways in which other people story their worlds too, the different storying styles that they employ in making sense of what's happening in their lives. Even reading - or as the case may be, re-reading - fables, fairy tales, or other stories that stood out for us from our childhood could take us deeper into our own stories. In fact, with two other colleagues (Randall, Achenbaum, & Lewis, in preparation), I've been revisiting old tales like *The Tortoise and The Hare* to see what meanings they might hold for me six decades since I first heard them or read them. How might they provide metaphors for themes in my life at various times across the years? In what ways have I been the tortoise, for instance, and in what ways, the hare?

Watching movies is another way of expanding our storyworlds. In fact, for many of us nowadays, this is the preferred mode of broadening our imaginative capacities. If we haven't experienced something directly ourselves - addiction, for example, or widowhood or cancer or the loss of a child - then we can have a sense of it vicariously at least, a reasonable facsimile thereof. We can *imagine* what that experience might feel like, and this can only enhance our ability to show empathy for that person's world, regardless of the differences - in gender, in culture, in age - that lie between us. So, then, listing the places we've lived, books we've enjoyed, movies we've savoured, music we love - any of these can heighten our awareness of the vastness of our own storyworld and widen the range of connections we can make with the worlds of others. In such a basic manner, taking narrative care of ourselves equips us better to take narrative care of them.

Other, more profound ways of taking narrative care of ourselves include keeping a journal. I think especially of the type of journaling that an Ira Progoff (1975) or a Tristine Rainer (1998) has promoted - in which we go beyond simply recording the events of our day to reflecting on what those events can teach us, the patterns that run through our memories, and the legacy of insight that's been silently amassing inside us. In his Intensive Journal Program, Progoff, for instance, advises us to begin preparing a "life history log" whereby "we gather all the facts of the past of our lives" (1975, p. 132). This then serves as raw material for a process of "philosophic deepening" (p. 12). Such deepening entails appreciating the "dynamic movement at the depth of ourselves" (p. 53), discerning "the inner myth that has been guiding our lives unknown to ourselves" (p. 11), and learning "to move around inside ourselves" (p. 99). Through something he calls "time-stretching" and through "dialogue" with different aspects of our lives (events, other people, our bodies, our dreams), we are enabled, he believes, to honour the "inner wisdom" that we each possess. It's like fostering a wisdom environment within ourselves!

Then there is writing, not a journal (however in-depth), but an actual memoir, and numerous resources have been published over the years heralding the therapeutic effects of exploring our own stories on paper. Among those I'm familiar with, though my list is admittedly outdated, Louise DeSalvo's (1999) book *Writing as a Way of Healing: How Telling Our Stories Transforms Our Lives* would be one. So is Mandy Aftel's (1996) *The Story of Your Life: Becoming the Author of Your Experience.* Dan Wakefield's (1990) book with the same main title, *The Story of Your Life: Writing as Spiritual Autobiography*, is the sort of resource that could be especially therapeutic for people working in the field of spiritual care. My friend, Karen Skerrett, a therapist herself, recently completed a memoir centred on her experience of being adopted as a child (Skerrett, 2018). Reflecting in an email to me on the difference between *writing* her story out and *talking* it out to someone in, say, a therapeutic context, here's how she explained things:

> *Clearly integration is an outcome of both processes, but ... writing seems more effective and meaningful. Some of it has to do with [McAdams'] notion of coherence ... writing out a storyline so that it holds together and taps some truth is different than telling the story in fits and starts with the therapist primarily holding the string (typically) and weaving the parts into coherence. There is also something about getting a storied experience out on paper that focuses attention, memory, and understanding in a unique way. Then, too, is the aspect ... [of] having another read it and reflect on your telling. That offers a whole new set of meanings on the story told ...*

One variation on memoir-writing that combines writing with reading and telling alike is what I mentioned briefly last chapter - guided autobiography - where a group of eight or nine people gather to look at their lives through the lens of broad life-themes like education, career, relationships, love, spirituality, and so forth (Birren & Deutchman, 1991; Birren & Cochran, 2001). From one session to another, each member of the group writes two pages about their life in relation to a given theme, then comes to the next meeting and reads them aloud to the others. In turn, they respond not by critiquing the writing - it's not that kind of group - but supportively, by asking questions for clarification. Then another member reads their two pages, and has it listened to and commented on in turn. In her comparative analyses of the experiences of older adults in writing groups versus reminiscence groups, narrative gerontologist, Kate de Medeiros (2011), says something similar to Skerrett, namely "that there is a difference in what is presented, what is emphasized, and how speakers/writers may modify their presentations on the basis of context, all of which point to *different presentations of self* (p. 173; emphasis mine).

Obviously, psychotherapy, spiritual direction, and indeed any sort of intentional exploration of the ins and outs of our inner world - all of these are excellent means of taking narrative care of ourselves, as are any of the other activities that I outlined in Chapter 7. A less time-consuming and, conveniently, more affordable means is, to use Patricia Hampl (1999) words, "listen[ing] to what our stories tell us" (p. 33). This is what I'd like to focus on now.

THE LEGEND OF THE IRON LUNG

At the end of his chapter on storytelling and storylistening, Jeffrey Kottler (2017) provides a list of questions that we can ask ourselves to, as he puts it, "dig into your own storied life" (p. 62). Among these are: "What is a story that had a powerful impact on your life?" "What is a significant experience in your life that you haven't yet formed into a coherent story?" - an untold story, if you will; a story - like the ones that those we counsel can have swirling around inside of them - that we don't know *how* to tell, that are knotted up inside of us, too deep for words, that we too might preface with a phrase like *I've never told this to anyone before*... Then, asks Kottler, "What is a story you frequently tell someone new that you meet, who you want to truly *know* you?" (p. 62) - the type of story I call a signature story, like my one about the iron lung that I referred to briefly back in Chapter 3. There's a comical coda to that tale, however, that is worth recounting here. But first the story itself ...

When I was two years old, I came down with polio, as did my two sisters, due to the pandemic that raged through the Maritime Provinces some 60 years ago. Donna nearly died from it, due to paralysis of the trachia, while Carol was left permanently disabled. As for me, the disease attacked my diaphragm. For two weeks early on, I was consigned to an iron lung. Without it, I would have died, unable to catch my breath. With it, I survived to tell the tale. In that tale, I am in a grey, sterile room with nothing else in it but me and the machine. No one else is around. It's not gaily papered with teddybears and smiley-faces like a children's ward today, but barren and drab. I even recall there being bars on the windows, outside of which swarmed the thick fog that often engulfed the seaside city where our family was living at the time.

Dismal as it sounds, I've always liked this little story - in fact, it's not so much a story as it is just an image in my head. Still, dozens of times across the years, I've heard myself recount it, often at social occasions when the conversation turns to topics of this type: occasions when a little sympathy can help you get your way, or at least get you some attention across the punch bowl. For I've always like how it portrays me: a tiny child-hero, powerless yet tough. For once, it makes me look good, not like all those other stories that I tell about myself where I come out looking like a chump. Here comes the coda, though.

The problem is, the story isn't true, or at least the bit about the iron lung. According to my aging parents, whose memory of the event I finally solicited some forty years further on, it never took place. True, I contracted polio, and true, they didn't treat it lightly when I contracted pneumonia later on. But that merely meant that I was put in an oxygen tent for a day or so. Not an iron lung. "Where did you get *that* idea?!?!" they asked me, amused, and then proceeded to imply, ever so politely, that I'd trumped the whole thing up. With equal politeness, I implied that they had done the same with *their* version, that being my parents didn't necessarily place them nearer the truth. Indeed, the truth, I even ventured, had needed doctoring because it was too hard for them to handle: that they had been powerless to assist me and, in my direst hour, had abandoned me to a machine.

In the end, I had to concede that my version of things was incorrect, to the point where I felt guilty almost and was tempted to track down all those to whom I'd told it and set the record straight. For, in good conscience, I can no longer recount it the same way that I used to, or if I do, then I'm obliged to add this coda. Which actually works well, of course, from a pedagogical perspective, because I can tell it now, not as a story per se, so much as a story *about* stories. It illustrates how autobiographical memory is frequently a matter of faction; how the stories around which we construct our identity - the material we gather in our pre-mythic years, for instance - commonly have questionable roots. At the same time, though, they can hold untold potential for meaning. They may be suspect in terms of their historical truth, yet be brimming with narrative truth - truth in terms of significance, not certainty.

With this story in mind, and most of us have comparable tales tucked away within our personal libraries, stories we have heard ourselves tell on countless occasions yet never really reflected on, I have followed Kottler's suit and generated a few questions of my own. For example: How does it feel to us to tell this story? In what situations do we tend to tell it, and why? What effect does it have on our listeners, or do we hope it has? How has our telling of it changed over time? And how have our feelings about it changed? How might we have stretched or embellished the central events? How do we characterize ourselves within it (victim, hero?), and how do we characterize others? Are there additional stories that this might be a cover for and that merit telling as well? What is *behind* this story, in other words? And what is *in* it? What is its main message, its principal themes, its meaning - or meanings - overall?

In the case of my iron lung story, I've wondered sometimes what meanings I can glean from it regarding my experience of the Randall family as a whole. Borrowing from a picture of an iron lung that I maybe came across in a book or magazine, did my imagination dream the whole thing up as a way of inflating the role that I played within the Randall family drama, compared to what Carol or Donna played? As for Donna in particular, her role has always stood out less clearly to me than Carol's, due to the care and attention that Carol's handicaps demanded from the rest of us, not to mention the formidable force of her personality itself.

Donna, a softer soul all around, whose world orbits about her own family now, left New Brunswick in her early 20s, never to return, except once or twice a year to visit. In a sense, she extracted herself from the convoluted emotional dynamics that have characterized interactions among the rest of us, many of them centred on the theme of guilt: survivor guilt, specifically - guilt for being able to run and play and ride a bike, unlike Carol; guilt for pulling through polio more or less intact. If, however, Donna had actually died from the disease (and she came closer to it than either Carol or I), then she would have extracted herself from the family drama once and for all, her death itself no doubt emerging thereafter as a dark but defining episode within it. In a sense, she and not Carol would have been the star of the show, clearly not me.

Is this, then, how the myth of the iron lung got its start, as a ploy to get the limelight shifted onto me instead? And still on the topic of Donna, what kind of character has she played in my story, and I in hers? What we-stories have she and I created and how do I feel about them? What sort of subplot has our relationship as a whole represented in each of our lives? How has it influenced the way my own story has unfolded and the sorts of themes with which it's been laced? How would it be different, for instance, if she had never been part of it at all? And, bigger question still, how would it be different if I had never had polio at all, iron long or not?

For my iron lung story has been a secret source of psychic strength, enabling me to see myself as a hero at heart, albeit a passive, long-suffering one, yet a hero all the same. Or at the very least, different. Like the ace that I've kept quietly up my sleeve, it has served me as a refuge, a shield, a line of last defence whenever my sense of self-worth has felt under assault. Which is why, when my parents called it so abruptly into question, when (basically) they took it away from me, like a security blanket is snatched from a child, I was taken aback. "How dare you?!" I wanted to retort. Yet I quickly recovered my composure, took the long view of things, and with an air of affectionate detachment, could appreciate the humour in the situation. Had they tried to set me straight 30 or 40 years prior, who knows? I might have reacted rather differently and, indeed, been permanently rattled. But at the time, at nearly 45, with accomplishments under my belt and a self-assurance that I'd been lacking in the past, I could bid fond farewell to my beloved iron lung, thankful for the countless times that I'd enlisted it to come to my aid.

It's clear, then, how much we can play with the possibilities that our stories contain, the questions they can raise for consideration, the way they can bring us full circle to a deepened understanding of our self and our life. "Play" is the operative word here, however, for it may be best to engage in these sorts of considerations in a gently ironic, light-hearted manner (Randall, 2013). But listening deeply to a fellow human being requires honouring the mystery not just in our signature stories, for they are often positive in nature and comparatively easy to relate, but in those stories that are not.

Our capacity to provide narrative care to others is rooted in our capacity to use every part of our storyworld as a possible point of entry into theirs. It is proportional to our capacity to harvest, to find the parabolic potential in, not just our successes but our failures as well, our lows as much as our highs, our questions as much as our convictions. It is dependent on our capacity to contemplate our signature stories for sure, but our secret stories too. It is dependent on what a little book entitled *The Slow Professor* refers to as our "shadow CV;" in other words, "the list of detours, delays, and abandoned projects that we hide" (Berg & Seeber, 2016, p. 65). It is dependent on the darker, riskier stories that we don't yet know how to tell; on the twisted subplots, the aborted adventures, the broken dreams, the lost threads, the lost loves, the dead ends, and the chopped-up chapters in our own life-narrative. For nothing is wasted, nothing is lost. All of it is grist for the mill, is grounds for compassion, and ultimately is just part of our story. And, in the end, our story may be all we have. More than our gains and achievements, it may well be in our loss and our pain - in the sacrament of failure - that lies the sacred tale of our own lives, too.

Postscript:
In Praise of Narrative Openness

*I enjoy talking to very old men, for they have gone before us ...
on a road that we too may have to tread,
and it seems to me that we should find out from them what it is like
and whether it is rough and difficult or broad and easy.
You are now at an age when you are, as the poets say,
about to cross the threshold.*
- Socrates to Cephalus (Plato, 1953, p. 62f)

*Our first question is not how to go out and help the elderly,
but how to allow the elderly to enter into the center of our own lives,
how to create the space where they can be heard and listened to from
within, with careful attention ... Care for the elderly means, first of all,
to make ourselves available to the experience of becoming old. ...
No guest will ever feel welcome when his host
is not at home in his own house.*
- Henri Nouwen & Walter Gaffney (1976, p. 101f)

When he was about the same age I was at the time I recited that naughty poem at Sunday dinner, my father's best friend was Grandfather Ring. After the death of the man's wife, my Nana's mother, he came to live with my father's family, as often happened before the days of nursing homes as we know them now. Dad's own father had a job as cook in a lumber camp deep in the Nova Scotia forest, so was absent from family life for weeks at a stretch. As for Dad's sister, my aunt Leah, she was 6 years older, and they were never particularly close at the best of times. So, with no brothers and with few lads his own age living nearby, Dad was, by his own admission, a somewhat lonely kid.

Grandfather Ring was 66 years older than Dad. That might seem like a lot, unless of course you consider that our bodies are made of cells, our cells are made of molecules, and our molecules are made of atoms. And since atoms are made in the hearts of stars, that means all of us are "billion-year-olds no matter when we were born," points out gerontologist Leonard Hayflick (1994), "and celebrating birthdays is absurd" (p. 18). Still, though 66 years might be nothing in the grand scheme of things, it was certainly not an obvious match. Yet the two of them worked together amicably at the various chores involved in running the family farm - milking cows, feeding chickens, cleaning pens, piling wood - and in the process, developed a marvellous connection. In Dad's words, "we were buddies."

He loved telling me how the two of them would talk back and forth as they went about their work, and how much he learned from these conversations, especially about family history, which evolved into one of Dad's abiding passions. And I loved listening to him tell me, for in the listening I found myself loving him all the more. It was one of those "nostalgic stories" (Synnes, 2015) that reminded him of the pleasanter aspects of his life growing up. And it was a teaching story too, a way of impressing on me the importance of having older people in our lives, not just as mentors but as friends - a point he took great pains to stress, I'm certain, when he spoke each year to Grade Two students as part of the Grandparents-In-School program. I know that every time I heard the story, I envied the relationship that the two of them enjoyed, for I felt that I'd missed out. My father's father passed away of Lou Gehrig's Disease the year before I was born, so I never knew him at all. As for my maternal grandfather, Grampie Benson, he lived in another part of Nova Scotia altogether so I only got to see him for a few days in the summer. Even then, I had to share his attention with my sisters.

One night, upstairs in his bedroom supposedly asleep, Dad listened in on his grandfather and mother as they chatted quietly by the kitchen stove. "I love all of my grandchildren," the man confided to her; "but I think young William is my favourite." Why is that?, Nana asked, curious. "Well, when I'm with the other ones, it's always 'Grampie, Grampie, look at me. Grampie, Grampie, look what I can do. Grampie, Grampie, guess what I learned today?!'. But with William it's different." Why's that?, Nana inquired once more, happy that her little boy held a special place in her father's heart. "Well," he replied, "rather than going on about *his* life, he asks me about *my* life instead. 'Grampie,' he'll say, 'tell me about what things were like when you were *my* age!' He gets me telling stories ..."

Older adults as storytellers, as storykeepers (David, 2004), as wisdomkeepers (Wall & Arden, 2006) - this theme has been implicit since the start. And Dad had an inherent awareness of it early on, thanks to Grampie Ring. Meanwhile, Grampie's golden years were obviously enriched as a result. They were key characters in the narratives of one another's lives, co-authors of them too, and for the time they were together, their stories were tightly entwined. It was a win-win arrangement, intergenerational interaction at its best.

True, the lives of older adults can be limited in many ways - mobility-wise, energy-wise, health-wise. And, true, their hearts can be filled with a sense of the tasks, of the slow questions, that aging is nudging them to address, well below the realm of words. But, as Dad learned from Grampie Ring, their hearts are filled with stories too. And their stories can be filled with insights. And their insights can enlighten us immensely, if only we will listen. For in listening closely to older adults' stories, in being open to what we can learn from them about all manner of things, including aging itself, we foster a safe space - a sacred space - where they can begin to feel valued, not just for being old but for being Elders too. And if ever our world needed the knowledge of its Elders to ground us, guide us, and curb our infatuation with a future that grows more frightening by the day, then the time is clearly now. In that space, in the wisdom environment that gets created between us, good things can happen - growth can happen - for teller and listener alike. We each find ways to keep our stories open.

I'd like to try and conclude my thinking in this book - if "conclusions" are ever possible where the topic of narrative is concerned - with a few further musings on this notion of narrative openness that I've talked about throughout.

I mentioned in a previous chapter that Dad had a temper that wasn't easy to be around, and you never knew what would set it off. The more often he told me about his friendship with Grampie Ring, however, the more I've forgiven him for those occasions when I bore its brunt. Grampie Ring was a person of fervent faith, and no doubt Dad's own faith was influenced by the faith-related themes that got inserted into their chats as they went about their chores. Yet, he had his failings too, as evidenced by this little story from *Guidelines to MY Ancestors* (Randall, 2004), which Dad assembled when he himself was 85.

One windy autumn afternoon, the two of them were carrying firewood from the woodshed to the back kitchen of the family home. The shed had no sill beneath it, though, which meant that it wasn't very level. So if you needed the door not to close shut on you whenever you went through it, you had to prop it open with a stick. I'll let Dad himself take up the narrative from here ...

> *As I was about to go into our back kitchen I heard a crash, and I knew what had happened. The wind had caught the door and freed it from its restraint. The door slammed Grandfather right across the knuckles as he was coming out of the woodhouse. Grandfather dropped his armload, picked up a stick of wood ... and in one vicious stroke hit the woodhouse door and split it from top to bottom! My first reaction was to laugh,*

but then Grandfather fell to his knees. I thought, "Oh, my goodness, Grandfather has been hurt!" I said, "Grampie, are you alright?" He was ... on his knees with his hands over his eyes, and he was crying. I said, "Where did you hurt yourself?" Grandfather looked up, tears streaming from his eyes. "Oh, William, William, the devil got me again! I lost my temper. Oh, I am so ashamed! I wonder if God will ever forgive me. I wonder if God will ever release me from the bondage of this terrible temper!" (p. 54f)

For all his piety, Grampie was not perfect. He had his problems. He had his demons. Whether rooted in his nature, his religion, or unresolved issues from who knows what corners of his past, there were conflicts coursing through his psyche that, as I imagine the man ninety years later, makes him that much more endearing to me. As it did to my father, affording him a genealogical perspective, a long view, on his own temperament too. It made the man human, transparent, open; still striving - in his 80s - to better himself, to mature, to grow up.

Grampie's embarrassment and shame are cast in a redeemable light, however, by these words from the psychologist Carl Jung (1976): "The serious problems in life," writes Jung, "are never fully solved. If ever they should appear to be so it is a sure sign that something has been lost. The meaning and purpose of a problem," he says, "seem to lie not in its solution but in our working at it incessantly. This alone preserves us from stultification and petrifaction" (p. 11f).

I've been saying all along that there is no built-in limit to our narrative development; that our lives, as texts, are interpretively open, philosophically open. Like a parable, they leave us us with questions to consider, problems to work at, insights to savour. Like the best stories tend to do, they leave lots of loose ends. They may achieve closure of sorts, but it is *open* closure, not closed (Taha, 1998-99, p 5). The question, however, is whether we have sufficient energy - or encouragement - to embrace this open-endedness.

In the last pages of his autobiography, composed when he was in his 80s and, itself, an excellent text on the topic of aging and spirituality, Jung (1963) gives expression to the openness that he himself experienced near the threshold of his life. He does so, however, not in a depressing way really, but with a hint of excitement almost, not unlike Scott-Maxwell (1968)'s assessment of aging as a time of discovery, while at the same time admitting that "I never understood myself less" (p. 125). "The older I have become," he admits, "the less I have understood or had insight into or known about myself" (Jung, 1963, p. 352). He continues in this vein in the very next paragraph, more than mindful, just like Grampie Ring, of his own internal contradictions:

> *I am astonished, disappointed, pleased with myself. I am distressed, depressed, rapturous. I am all of these things at once, and cannot add up the sum. ... I have no judgment about myself and my life. There is nothing I am quite sure about. ... I know only that I was born and exist, and it seems to me that I have been carried along. I exist on the foundation of something I do not know. In spite of all uncertainties, I feel a solidity underlying all existence and a continuity in my mode of being.* (p. 358)

In an essay entitled "the stages of life," Jung (1976) offers his now famous observation that "we cannot live the afternoon of life according to the program of the morning" (p. 17). Indeed, he says, "the afternoon of human life must also have a significance of its own and cannot be merely a pitiful appendage to life's morning." The afternoon, Jung believes, brings it own set of duties and tasks. "[F]or the ageing person," he says, "it is a duty and a necessity to devote serious attention to himself" (p. 17).

But is Jung expecting too much of later life? For that matter, am *I* expecting too much? In some ways, I may be. Addressing the tasks that I've listed and challenges I've noted could seem something of a luxury, reserved for the educated elite; more than most older adults can handle, or be expected to handle, particularly those in "deep old age," for whom "narrative identity, version light" may, in fact, suffice. I can accept this concern. I can even support it, insofar as narrative care, however light, can still help to strengthen people's stories to whatever extent is possible. My own concern, though, is that we end up succumbing to what may well be just another form of ageism. Disguised as compassion, it sees aging, at bottom, in a negative light - our own aging included. My concern is that our expectations of later life have been unduly lowered by the narrative of decline, according to which aging is a downward drift toward decrepitude and death. It does not involve development in any real way but merely denouement. It is a matter of *getting* old, and little more. The vision of aging as a matter of *growing* old is all but eclipsed, and along with it that of older adults as Elders. We are right to expect more.

In *From Ageing to Sageing: A Profound New Vision of Growing Older*, Schacter-Shalomi expresses a similar concern in drawing attention to the philosophic homework that, regardless of our experience or education, aging nudges us to undertake (Schachter-Shalomi & Miller, 1995). He views this, however, not as "a shallow, academic exercise" but as "a passionate inquiry," its aim being "to synthesize wisdom from long life experience" (p. 124). One of the main avenues into this homework, I continue to believe, is through our own lifestories. For it is in our stories, it is in reading our lives, that our own brand of wisdom is to be found (Randall & Kenyon, 2001) - wisdom, though, that is less about arriving at hard and fast conclusions than about "staying loose," about "keeping our options open" (Bruner & Kalmar, 1996, p.), about seeing our life "as an evolving story" and reflecting on it "from multiple perspectives" (Ray, 2000, p. 29). That said, the word *homework* can be off-putting in itself: something to delay doing as long as we can, if not weasel out of altogether. But in contexts other than educational ones, homework is something we frequently can't wait to do, if we want something badly enough, that is - like buy a new vehicle, or build the house of our dreams, or prepare to take a trip to some exotic destination.

Perhaps this is the point. Wherever each of us may be along it, whether nearing its end or just setting out, we are all on the proverbial journey of life. And on that journey, which is always a journey inward as well, life invites us to accompany one another. It invites us to become *story companions*. The words of William Carlos Williams come to mind yet again: "Their stories, yours, mine," he advises the young Doctor Coles (1989), "it's what we all carry with us on this trip we take, and we owe it to each other to respect our stories and learn from them" (p. 30).

Sooner or later, good stories end. Yet there is no end to the meanings we can glean from them, the things that we can learn. In a sense, they raise more questions than they resolve, which is why we value them as dearly as we do. The stories of our lives are no exception. Interpretively, philosophically, spiritually, they are as open as open can be. This book, I like to think, has been open in similar ways, stirring up as many issues as it may have settled but, in the process, inspiring fresh insights into the links between aging, spirituality, and narrative. In so doing, I hope it will be of some assistance to those who aim to age as wisely and resiliently as they can, and, equally important, to those whose soulful calling it is to listen to them and learn - and, in the listening, care.

Appendices

APPENDIX 1

Strategies for Storylistening

excerpted with permission from
*Restorying Our Lives: Personal Growth Through
Autobiographical Reflection*
by Gary Kenyon and William Randall
(1997, pp. 139-141)

1. Listen with respect for the novelty of the other person's lifestory, for the rich texture of their unique tale. Listen with openness for how interesting they really are, and let them know you find them so, for this itself can empower them. Listen despite the storyotypes you are bound to build around them. In other words, listen for the ways that their story is sure to press buttons in your story, but resist reacting in your usual way because of that. This means: Be in touch with the vastness and complexity of your own story, and be open to learning more about it as you learn about theirs.

2. Listen with respect for the power of respectful, non-judging listening to open a space for them to restory in safety, to find new meanings in their own lifestory material, and to test out a different version of themselves than what they have told--and lived--in the past. At the same time, listen with respect for the resistance they may have to being listened to, for their resistance to being restoried. And listen with respect for the direction that they, not you, want to go with the telling. Be mindful of the fact that they are letting you listen at all, that they are trusting you enough to let you hear their tale.

3. Listen for the form of their self-telling as much as for its content. Do not get so caught up with the content that you miss the form. Listen for *how* they talk about themselves as much as for *what* they say. Listen for the actual words they

use, the tell-tale expressions, the vocabulary and tone, the recurring metaphors and figures of speech. Listen for the genre in which the telling seems to be done, for their characteristic storying style, and for the ways their words are reinforced (or belied) by their gestures, actions, or eyes.

4. Listen for how they characterize themselves, as well as others, amidst the circumstances and relationships they relate. Listen for hints of the guiding myth that underlies their sense of self. Listen for the themes that run through their anecdotes, and how these are handled, the philosophy of life to which they point.

5. Listen for the plot-lines by which the events they recount are connected, the main turning-points on which they turn, and the conflicts they reflect. Listen for the *sub*-plot-lines and even *counter*-plot-lines that run through their accounts. Listen for how such elements--plot, theme, character, genre--interact and intertwine in both the telling and (possibly) the living of their lives.

6. Listen for clues concerning the different larger stories in which their personal ones have been set. Listen for indications of the particular poetic structure, narrative environment, and kind of co-authoring that have been characteristic of each, for how these have shaped their values and views and directed or restricted their self-creation. Listen for the key events, characters, conflicts, turning-points, that have been pivotal in each.

7. Listen for what they do *not* say as much as for what they do, though listen with respect and not to pry. Listen for what is in the silences: the missing details, omitted events, unmentioned characters and themes--and be alert to the significance of such omissions, for the secrets to which they may point. Listen for the stories they leave untold, for the holes in their stories, for the stories within their stories, for the one story behind the many, for the text beneath the text,

or the *sub*text. Listen for hints of other stories that could be told if respectfully coaxed. Listen for the stories they *like* to tell--their signature stories--and those they keep to themselves. Above all, listen for the emotions in their stories, and the stories behind their emotions.

8. Listen not to change their lifestory or fix it, which could be to wrest it unfairly from them and, in a sense, *de*-story them. Rather, listen to enlarge their story, to expand and deepen it, thus "releasing the energy bound within it" (Houston, 1987, p. 99) and helping to increase their respect for their own storied depths.

9. Listen with concern to elicit less the 'true' story than a coherent or plausible one. Do not disregard the 'truth' issue entirely, but be aware that such (historical) truth is in any case not attainable, and that even if it were, it is ultimately not as relevant as 'narrative truth'. In other words, their lifestory, even if it plays loose with what you guess to be 'the facts', can still be the vehicle of truth, though of the type we encounter in a movie or novel or dream--a point one Alzheimer researcher has convincingly stressed (Crisp, 1995). At the same time, listen with alertness for the inevitable 'gaps' between the levels of their lifestory--outside, inside, and so on--or between what they tell you with their words and, again, show you with their gestures, actions, or eyes.

10. Listen for the type and degree of meaning-making they are inclined, or can be encouraged, to do. Listen with a view to helping them find more and newer meanings than they have made in the past, aware that their lives, like any good story, are infinitely meaning*ful*.

11. Listen less for the facts of their lives than for the interpretations they place upon them. And listen for the beginnings of different, possibly more positive interpretations, for alternative versions (*sub*-versions), that may be trying to break out between the lines of what they are

saying, versions you could midwife into being, thus putting a perhaps previously unimagined spin on the stuff of their life, which means opening the door for a new version of who they are.

12. Finally, listen not just to help *them* learn, but to learn *from them* Listen with openness for the message, wisdom, or truth that their lifestories uniquely embody. Listen in awe of the fact that in the exchange between you, a new lifestory, and thus a new life, is being co-authored - both for them and, potentially, for you.

APPENDIX 2

Quotes for Reflection

Over the years, I've been a collector of quotes. I sometimes fear that anything I've published is really just a smattering of quotations that I've managed to string together in a manner that will appear logical to the reader, thus fooling them into thinking that I know what I'm talking about! Even when taken out of the text in which they originally appear, certain quotations do seem, though, to stand on their own. They can set the mind spinning with fresh insights and questions - in the context of this book, insights and questions concerning the narrative complexity of human aging. In addition to those with which the book is already laced, it's my pleasure to include a few more of them here.

Every person is born into life as a blank page
- every person leaves life as a full book.
(Christina Baldwin)

Everyone's life is worth a novel.
(Gustave Flaubert)

If we wish to know a man, we ask "what is his story - his real, inmost story?" - for each of us is a biography, a story.
(Oliver Sacks)

We dream in narrative, daydream in narrative, remember, anticipate, hope, despair, believe, doubt, plan, revise, criticize, construct, gossip, learn, hate, and love in narrative.
(Barbara Hardy)

If all we know about ourselves is a story, what is to say that one story is superior to another?
(David Polonoff)

Stories happen to people who can tell them.
(Henry James)

*We turn our pain into narrative so we can bear it; we turn our ecstasy into narrative so we can prolong it.
... We tell our stories to live.*
(John Shea)

A man is always a teller of tales; he lives surrounded by his stories and the stories of others; he sees everything that happens to him through them, and he tries to live his life as if he were recounting it.
(Jean-Paul Sartre)

Ultimately, the richest resource for meaning and healing is one we already possess. It rests (mostly untapped) in the material of our own lifestory, in the sprawling, many-layered 'text' that has been accumulating within us across the years, weaving itself in the depths of, and as, our life.
(Gary Kenyon & William Randall)

A life is not "how it was" but how it is interpreted and reinterpreted, told and retold. ... A life as lived is inseparable from a life as told. ... In the end, we become the autobiographical narratives by which we 'tell about' our lives.
(Jerome Bruner)

The unexamined life is not worth living.
(Socrates)

We make stories about the world and to a large degree live out their plots.
(Carol Pearson)

As we grow older, it seems to be more important to look back than to look forward, to see our life in all its dimensions as a story. This shift in perspective starts for most of us in our forties and fifties. ... storying our lives plays a crucial role in personal development and should be taken seriously.
(Richard Stone)

Knowledge can only be genuinely transitional if it is biographical knowledge. The main issue is to decipher the surplus meanings of our biographical knowledge, and that in turn means to perceive the potentiality of our unlived lives. ... Unlived life does indeed possess socially explosive force.
(Peter Alheit)

Each moment in a person's life hosts an endless number of events. Considering the abundance of this treasure, relatively few stories emerge.
(Erving Polster)

Biographical self-reflection ... can take place naturally and spontaneously in adult education if the atmosphere and work methods are not strongly deterring it. ... there is no educational material, no subject matter, that would not be able to trigger any biographical self-reflection at all. ... Very often this biographical self-reflection happens under the "surface" of the learning process at the same time.
(Wilhelm Mader)

The process of autobiographical reflection (is) a fundamentally metaphorical one. A new relationship is being created between the past and present, a new poetic configuration, designed to give greater form to one's previous - and present - experience. The text of the self is thus being rewritten.
(Mark Freeman)

We are what we remember ourselves to be.
(Edward Casey)

Story is a tool for making us whole; stories gather up the parts of us and put them together in a way that gives our lives greater meaning than they had before we told our story.
(Robert Atkinson)

[Narrative foreclosure is] the conviction that the story of one's life ... has effectively ended. ... At an extreme, narrative foreclosure may lead to a kind of living death or even suicide, the presumption being that the future is a foregone conclusion, ... that it is simply too late to live meaningfully and that, consequently, there is little left to do but play out the prescribed ending.
(Mark Freeman)

Memories can cut both ways - they can depress us or elevate our spirit; they can bind us or set us free.
(Paul Wong)

... the greatest stories have never been told; they lie under cemetery stones or have turned to dust or sand.
(Leon Surmelian)

We tell ourselves stories of our past, make fictions or stories of it, and these narrations become the past, the only part of our lives that is not submerged.
(Carolyn Heilbrun)

Each one of us makes for himself an illusion of a world - poetic, sentimental, joyful, melancholic, ugly or gloomy according to his nature.
(Guy de Maupassant)

Because we are engaged in a day-by-day process of self-invention ... both the past and the future are raw material, shaped and reshaped by each individual.
(Mary Catherine Bateson)

Memory is a great artist.
(André Maurois)

There can be different "versions" of the story of one's life, each presenting a different text for interpretation.
(Stuart Charmé)

[Memory is] a densely written text ... inextricably interwoven with the countless texts and contexts of culture. It is part of an infinite intertext that stretches out not only into the present but also into the past .... personal memory [is] just one moment in the endless and beginningless space of history & historical knowledge, autobiographical consciousness covers only a tiny island of awareness, temporarily surfacing from a sea of unknown & unknowable size.
(Jens Brockmeier)

Too often, as children, we are encouraged to try to be something other than ourselves. It is demanded that we assume a character not our own, live out a life story written by another. The plot is given. Improvisations are unacceptable. Neurosis is in part the result of being miscast into a scenario plotted out in accord with someone else's unfulfilled dreams and unfaced anxieties.
(Sheldon Kopp)

... memory, trickster figure, will let you down - a fiction writer offering alternate versions of what you had once imagined written in stone: the immutable facts of your life.
(P. K. Page)

Our memories are the fragile but powerful products of what we recall from the past, believe about the present, and imagine about the future.
(Daniel Schacter)

Memory is where the self is held captive. Telling one's story is a means of becoming.
(Ruthellen Josselson & Amia Lieblich)

We live immersed in narrative, recounting and reassessing the meanings of our past actions, anticipating the outcomes of future projects, situating ourselves at the intersection of several stories not yet completed.
(Donald Polkinghorne)

When it comes to our lifestories, nothing is ever final. Things can always change.
(Dan McAdams)

A lifestory is an open unit... whose structure is not tightly constrained ... [and] which is both structurally and interpretively open. ... A lifestory necessarily changes constantly - by the addition of stories about new events, by the loss of certain old stories, and by the reinterpretation of old stories to express new evaluations. We change our stories at least slightly for each new audience; we change a given story for a given addressee as our relation to that addressee changes; we reshape stories as new events occur and as we acquire new values that change our understanding of past events; and we change our stories as our point of view, our ideology, or our overall understanding changes and reshapes our history.
(Charlotte Linde)

Life stories must mesh within a community of stories; tellers and listeners must share some "deep structure" about the nature of a "life," for if the rules of life-telling are altogether arbitrary, tellers and listeners will surely be alienated by a failure to grasp what the other is saying or what he thinks the other is hearing.
(Jerome Bruner)

We only store in memory images of value. ... this, we say somewhere deep within us, is something I'm hanging onto. ... What is remembered is what becomes reality.
(Patricia Hampl)

When we write an autobiography we move from the known to the unknown; we attempt to grasp the unknown, the mystery of the self, through the known, the myriad details of the story of one's own life. The details are not the self, but they ought to point to it, be a metaphor of it. ... Like a parable, an autobiography tells a particular kind of story, a metaphorical story ... the autobiography is intended to be a metaphor of the self.
(Sallie TeSelle)

People think in terms of stories. They understand the world in terms of stories that they have already understood. New events or problems are understood by reference to old previously understood stories and explained to others by the use of stories. We understand personal problems and relationships between people through stories that typify those situations. ... Scientists have prototypical scientific success and failure stories that they use to help them with new problems. Historians have their favourite stories in terms of which they understand and explain the world. Stories are very basic to the human thinking process.
(Roger Schank)

At the end of our lives, after we have passed on, all that is left of us is our story.
(Richard Stone)

References

Abbott, H. (2002). *The Cambridge introduction to narrative.* New York: Cambridge University Press.

Adams, D. (1979). *The hitchhiker's guide to the galaxy.* London: Pan.

Aftel, M. (1996). *The story of your life: Becoming the author of your experience.* New York: Simon & Schuster.

Alheit, P. (1995). Biographical learning: Theoretical outline, challenges, and contradictions of a new approach in adult education. In P. Alheit, A. Bron-Wojciechowska, E. Brugger, & P. Dominice (Eds.), *The biographical approach in European adult education* (pp. 57-74). Vienna: Verband Wiener Voksbildung.

Andrews, M. (2014). *Narrative imagination and everyday life.* New York: Oxford University Press.

Atkinson, R. (1995). *The gift of stories: Practical and spiritual applications of autobiography, life stories, and personal mythmaking.* Westport, CT: Bergin & Garvey.

Atwood, M. (1996). *Alias Grace.* Toronto, ON: Doubleday.

Baldwin, C. (2006). The narrative dispossession of people living with dementia: Thinking about the theory and method of narrative. In K. Milnes, C. Horrocks, N. Kelly, B. Roberts, & D. Robinson (Eds.), *Narrative, memory, and knowledge: Representations, aesthetics, and contexts* (pp. 101-109). Huddersfield, UK: University of Huddersfield.

Baldwin, C. (2015). Narrative ethics for narrative care. *Journal of Aging Studies. 34.* 183-189.

Baldwin, C. (2005). *Storycatcher: Making sense of our lives through the power and practice of story.* Novato, CA: New World Library.

Baldwin, C., & Estey, J. (2015). The self and spirituality: Overcoming narrative loss in aging. *Journal of Aging and Spirituality in Social Work, 34*(2). 205-222.

Barr, J. (1984). *Escaping from fundamentalism.* London: SCM.

Basting, A. (2003). Reading the story behind the story: Context and content in stories by people with dementia. *Generations: The Journal of the American Society on Aging, 23*(3): 25-29.

Bateson, M. (1989). *Composing a life.* New York: Atlantic Monthly Press.

Bateson, M. (2007). Narrative, adaptation, change. *Interchange, 38*(3), 213-222.

Baur, S. (1994). *Confiding: A psychotherapist and her patients search for stories to live by*. New York: HarperPerennial.

Beardslee, W. (1990). Stories in the postmodern world: Orienting and disorienting. In D. Griffin (Ed.), *Sacred interconnections: Postmodern spirituality, political economy, and art* (pp. 163-175). Albany, NY: State University of New York Press.

Berendonk, C., Blix, B., Randall, W., Baldwin, C., & Caine, V. (2017). Care as narrative practice in the context of long term care: Theoretical considerations. *International Journal of Older People's Nursing.* 1-9.

Berg, M., & Seeber, B. (2016). *The slow professor: Challenging the culture of speed in the academy*. Toronto: University of Toronto Press.

Berger, P. (1963). *Invitation to sociology: A humanistic perspective*. Garden City, NY: Anchor.

Berman, H. (1994). *Interpreting the aging self: Personal journals of later life*. New York: Springer.

Berry, T. (1987). The new story: Comments on the origin, identification, and transmission of values. *Cross Currents, 37*(2-3). 187-199.

Birren, J., & Cochran, K. (2001). *Telling the stories of life through guided autobiography*. Baltimore, MD: Johns Hopkins University Press.

Birren, J., & Deutchman, D. (1991). *Guiding autobiography groups for older adults: Exploring the fabric of life*. Baltimore: The Johns Hopkins University Press.

Blythe, R. (1979). *The view in winter: Reflections on old age*. London: Penguin.

Bohlmeijer, E., Kramer, J., Smit, F., Onrust, S., & Marwijk, H. (2009). The effects of integrative reminiscence on depressive symptomatology and mastery of older adults. *Journal of Community Mental Health, 45*, 467-484.

Bohlmeijer, E., Valenkamp, M., Westerhof, G., Smit, G., & Cuijpers, P. (2005). Creative reminiscence as an early intervention for depression: Results of a pilot project. *Aging & Mental Health, 9*(4), 302-304.

Bohlmeijer, E., & Westerhof, G. (2011). Reminiscence interventions: Bringing narrative gerontology into practice. In G. Kenyon, E. Bohlmeijer, & W. Randall (Eds.), *Storying later life: Issues, investigations, and interventions in narrative gerontology.* (pp. 273-289). New York: Oxford University Press.

Bohlmeijer, E., Westerhof, G., Randall, W., Tromp, T., & Kenyon, G. (2011). Narrative foreclosure: Preliminary considerations for a new sensitizing concept. *Journal of Aging Studies, 25*(4). 364-370.

Boisen, A. (1936). *The exploration of the inner world: A study of mental disorder and religious experience.* New York: Harper & Brothers.

Bridges, W. (1980). *Transitions: Making sense of life's changes.* Toronto: Addison-Wesley.

Brooks, P. (1985). *Reading for the plot: Design and intention in narrative.* New York: Vintage.

Bruner, J. (1986). *Actual minds, possible worlds.* Cambridge, MA: Harvard University Press.

Bruner, J. (1987). Life as narrative. *Social Research, 5,4* (1). 11-32.

Bruner, J. (1990). *Acts of meaning.* Cambridge, MA: Harvard University Press.

Bruner, J. (1999). Narratives of aging. *Journal of Aging Studies, 13*(1), 7-9.

Bruner, J., & Kalmar, D. (1998). Narrative and metanarrative in the construction of the self. In M. Ferrari & R. Sternberg (Eds.), *Self-awareness: Its nature and development* (pp. 308-331). New York, NY: Guilford.

Butala, S. (2005). The memoirist's quandary. *McGill Journal of Education, 40*(1), 43-54.

Butler, R. (1963). The life review: An interpretation of reminiscence in the aged. *Psychiatry, 26.* 65-76.

Carstensen, L., Isaacowitz, D., & Charles, S. (1999). Taking time seriously: A theory of socioemotional selectivity. *American Psychologist, 54.* 165-181.

Carstensen, L., & Mikels, J. (2005). At the intersection of emotion and cognition: Aging and the positivity effect. *Current Directions in Psychological Science, 14.* 117-121.

Chandler, S., & Ray, R. (2002). New meanings for old tales: A discourse-based study of reminiscence and development in later life. In J. Webster & B. Haight (Eds.), *Critical advances in reminiscence work: From theory to application* (pp. 76-94). New York: Springer.

Charmé, S. (1984). *Meaning and myth in the study of lives: A Sartrean perspective.* Philadelphia: University of Pennsylvania Press.

Charon, R. (2006). *Narrative medicine: Honoring the stories of illness.* New York: Oxford University Press.

Chopra, D. (2014). *The future of God: A practical approach to spirituality for our times.* New York: Harmony.

Coelho, P. (1997). *The alchemist.* London: Harper.

Cohen, D. (2010). *Music and memory.* www.musicandmemory.org

Cohen, G. (2005). *The mature mind: The positive power of aging brain.* Boston: Basic Books.

Cole, T. (1992). *The journey of life: A cultural history of aging in America.* New York: Cambridge University Press.

Coleman, P. (1999). Creating a life story: The task of reconciliation. *The Gerontologist, 39*(2), 133-139.

Coles, R. (1989). *The call of stories: Teaching and the moral imagination.* Boston: Houghton Mifflin.

Connor, K., & Davidson, J. (2003). Development of a new resilience scale: The Connor-Davidson Resilience Scale (CD-RISC). *Depression and Anxiety, 18.* 71-82.

Crisp, J. (1995). Making sense of the stories that people with Alzheimer's tell: A journey with my mother. *Nursing Inquiry, 2*: 133–140.

Crossan, J. D. (1975). *The dark interval: Towards a theology of story.* Niles, IL: Argus Communications.

David, J. (2004). *Story keepers: Conversations with Aboriginal writers.* Owen Sound, ON: Ningwakwe Learning Press.

Denzin, N. (1997). *Interpretive ethnography: Ethnographic practices for the 21st century.* Thousand Oaks, CA: Sage.

DeSalvo, L. (1999). *Writing as a way of healing: How telling our stories transforms our lives.* Boston, MA: Beacon.

Draaisma, D. (2006). *Why life speeds up as you get older: How memory shapes our past.* Cambridge, UK: Cambridge University Press.

Eakin, P. J. (1999). *How our lives become stories: Making selves.* Ithaca, NY: Cornell University Press.

Erikson, E. (1963). *Childhood and society* (2nd edition). New York: W. W. Norton.

Erikson, E., Erikson, J., & Kivnick, H. (1986). *Vital involvement in old age.* New York: W. W. Norton.

Ferguson, N. (1997). Introduction: Virtual history: Towards a "chaotic" theory of the past. In N. Ferguson (Ed.), *Virtual history: Alternatives and counterfactuals* (pp. 1-90). London: Papermac.

Fireman, G., McVay, T., & Flanagan, O. (Eds.) (2003). *Narrative and consciousness: Literature, psychology, and the brain.* New York: Oxford University Press.

Fivush, R. (1994). Constructing narrative, emotion, and gender in parent-child conversations about the past. In U. Neisser & R. Fivush (eds.), *The remembering self: Construction and accuracy of the life narrative* (pp. 136-157). New York: Cambridge University Press.

Flynn, D. (1991). Community as story: A comparative study of community in Canada, England, and the Netherlands. *The Rural Sociologist,* Spring. 24-35.

Fowler, J. (1981). *Stages of faith: The psychology of human development and the quest for meaning.* San Francisco: Harper & Row.

Frank, A. (2010). *Letting stories breathe: A socio-narratology.* Chicago, IL: University of Chicago Press.

Freedman, J., & Combs, G. (1996). *Narrative therapy: The social construction of preferred realities.* New York: W. W. Norton.

Freeman, M. (1994). *Rewriting the self: History, memory, narrative.* London: Routledge.

Freeman, M. (1997). Death, narrative integrity, and the radical challenge of self-understanding: A reading of Tolstoy's *Death of Ivan Ilych*. *Ageing and Society, 17*: 373-398.

Freeman, M. (2000). When the story's over: Narrative foreclosure and the possibility of self-renewal. In M. Andrews, S. Slater, C. Squire, & A. Treacher (Eds.), *Lines of narrative: Psychosocial perspectives* (pp. 81-91). London: Routledge.

Freeman, M. (2002). Charting the narrative unconscious: Cultural memory and the challenge of autobiography. *Narrative Inquiry, 12*(1), 193-211.

Freeman, M. (2010). *Hindsight: The promise and peril of looking backward.* New York: Oxford University Press.

Freeman, M. (2011). Narrative foreclosure in later life: Possibilities and limits. In G. Kenyon, E. Bohlmeijer, & W. Randall (Eds.), *Storying later life: Issues, investigations, and interventions in narrative gerontology* (pp. 3-19). New York: Oxford University Press.

Friedan, B. (1993). *The fountain of age.* New York: Simon & Schuster.

Fry, P., & Keyes, C. (Eds.) (2010). *New frontiers in resilient aging: Life-strengths and well-being in late life.* New York: Cambridge University Press.

Frye, N. (1980). *The great code: The Bible and literature.* Toronto, ON: Academic Press Canada.

Fulford, R. (1999). *The triumph of narrative: Storytelling in an age of mass culture.* Toronto, ON: Anansi Press.

Furlong, D., Randall, W., Baldwin, C., McKenzie-Mohr, S., & McKim, E. (2015). The importance of the stories of others: Narrative embeddedness as a feature of resilience. Paper for *Canadian Association on Gerontology*, Calgary, AB. October 23.

Gardner, D. (1997). New perspectives: Stories and life stories in therapy with older adults. In K. Dwivedi (Ed.), *The therapeutic use of stories* (pp. 211-226). London: Routledge.

Gardner, H. (1990). *Frames of mind: The theory of multiple intelligences.* San Francisco, CA: Basic Books.

Gold, J. (2002). *The story species: Our life-literature connection.* Markham, ON: Fitzhenry & Whiteside.

Goldberg, M. (1991). *Theology and narrative: A critical introduction.* Philadelphia, PA: Trinity Press International.

Goolishian, H. (1990). Therapy as a linguistic system: Hermeneutics, narrative and meaning. *The Family Psychologist 6*, 44-45.

Gordon, K. (2003). The impermance of being: Toward a psychology of uncertainty. *Journal of Humanistic Psychology, 43*(2): 96-117.

Grams, A. (2001). Learning, aging, and other predicaments. In S. McFadden & R. Atchley (Eds.), *Aging and the meaning of time: A multidisciplinary exploration* (pp. 99-110). New York: Springer.

Gubrium, J. (1993). *Speaking of life: Horizons of meaning for nursing home residents.* Hawthorne, NY: Aldine de Gruyter.

Guest, E. (1916). When you know a fellow. In *A heap o'livin' along life's highway* (pp. 11-12). Chicago: The Reilly & Lee Co.

Gullette, M. (2004). *Aged by culture.* Chicago, IL: University of Chicago Press.

Habermas, T. (2019). *Emotion and narrative: Perspectives on autobiographical storytelling.* Cambridge, UK: Cambridge University Press.

Habermas, T. (2010). Autobiographical reasoning: Arguing and narrating from a biographical perspective. *New Directions for Child and Adolescent Development, 131.* (pp. 1-17). San Francisco, CA: Jossey-Bass.

Hamkins, S. (2014). *The art of narrative psychiatry: Stories of strength and meaning.* New York: Oxford University Press.

Hammerskjöld, D. (1964). *Markings* (I. Sjöberg & W Auden, Trans.). New York: Ballantine.

Hampl, P. (1999). *I could tell you stories: Sojourns in the land of memory.* New York: W. W. Norton.

Hauerwas, S. (1977). *Truthfulness and tragedy: Further investigations into Christian ethics.* Notre Dame, IN: University of Notre Dame Press.

Hauerwas, S., & Jones, L. G. (Eds.). (1989). *Why narrative?: Readings in narrative theology.* Grand Rapids, MI: William B. Eerdmans.

Haught, J. (1984). *The cosmic adventure: Science, religion, and the quest for purpose.* New York: Paulist.

Haught, J. (2017) *The new cosmic story: Inside our awakening universe.* New Haven, CT: Yale University Press.

Hayflick, L. (1994). *How and why we age.* New York: Ballantine.

Hedelund, M., & Nikolajsen, A. (2013). *Tell stories for life: Articulation and verification of a poststructuralist and narrative praxis concerning storytelling with old people.* Unpublished Master's Thesis, Department of Psychology, University of Copenhagen.

Herman, D. (2002). *Story logic: Problems and possibilities of narrative.* Lincoln, NB: University of Nebraska Press.

Hermans, H. (2000). Meaning as movement: The relativity of the mind. In G. Reker & K. Chamberlain (Eds.), *Exploring existential meaning: Optimizing human development across the lifespan* (pp. 23-38). Thousand Oaks, CA: Sage.

Hillman, J. (1975). The fiction of case history: A round. In J. Wiggins (Ed.), *Religion as story* (pp. 123-173). New York: Harper & Row.

Holmes, O. (2005). The chambered nautilus. In *The Poetical Works of Oliver Wendell Holmes.* Whitefish, MT: Kessinger. (Original work published 1895.)

Hopewell, J. F. (1987). *Congregation: Stories and structures.* Philadelphia, PA: Fortress Press.

Hydén, L.-C. (2017). *Entangled narratives: Collaborative storytelling and the re-imagining of dementia.* New York: Oxford University Press.

Johnston, R. (August 20, 2014). Meeting God at the movies: Film as a source of revelation. *The Christian Century*, 24-27.

Josselson, R. (2020). *Narrative and cultural humility: Reflections from "the good witch" teaching psychotherapy in China.* New York: Oxford University Press.

Jourard, S. (1971). *The transparent self.* New York: Litton.

Jung, C. G. (1963). *Memories, dreams, and reflections.* New York: Vintage.

Jung, C. G. (1976). The stages of life. In J. Campbell (Ed.), *The portable Jung* (pp. 3-22). London: Penguin

Kazin, A. (1981). The self as history: Reflections on autobiography. In A. E. Stone (Ed.), *The American autobiography: A collection of critical essays*, (pp. 31-43). Englewood Cliffs, NJ: Prentice-Hall.

Keen, S., & Fox, A. (1974). *Telling your story: A guide to who you are and who you can be.* Toronto, ON: New American Library.

Kennedy, E. (1972). *On becoming a counselor. A basic guide for non-professional counselors.* New York: Continuum.

Kenyon, G., Bohlmeijer, E., & Randall, W. (Eds.) (2011). *Storying later life: Issues, investigations, and interventions in narrative gerontology.* New York: Oxford University Press.

Kenyon, G., & Randall, W. (1997). *Restorying our lives: Personal growth through autobiographical reflection.* Westport, CT: Praeger.

Kermode, F. (1966). *The sense of an ending: Studies in the theory of fiction.* New York: Oxford University Press.

King, T. (2003). *The truth about stories: A native narrative.* Toronto, ON: Anansi.

Kleinman, A. (1988). *The illness narratives: Suffering, healing, and the human condition.* New York: Basic Books.

Koenig, G. (1995). Religion and health in later life. In M. Kimble, S. McFadden, J. Ellor, & J. Seeber, (Eds.), *Aging, spirituality, and religion: A handbook* (pp. 9-29). Minneapolis, MN: Augsburg Fortress.

Kottler, J. (2017). *On being a therapist* (5th edition). New York: Oxford University Press.

Kotre, J. (1984). *Outliving the self: Generativity and the interpretation of lives.* Baltimore, MD: Johns Hopkins University Press.

Kotre, J. (1999). *Make it count: How to generate a legacy that gives meaning to your life.* New York: Free Press.

Kramer, D. (1983). Post formal operations? A need for further conceptualization. *Human Development 26*, 91-105.

Kropf, N., & Tandy, C. (1998). Narrative therapy with older clients: The use of a "meaning-making" approach. *Clinical Gerontologist. 18(4).* 3-16.

Kuhl, D. (2002). *What dying people want: Practical wisdom for the end of life.* Toronto: Doubleday.

Labouvie-Vief, G. (2000). Positive development in later life. In T. Cole, R. Kastenbaum, & R. Ray (Eds.), *Handbook of the humanities and aging* (2nd ed.), (pp. 365-380). New York: Springer.

de Lange, F. (2015). *Loving later life: An ethics of aging.* Grand Rapids, MI: Eerdmans.

de Lange, F. (2011). Inventing yourself: How older adults deal with the pressure of late-modern identity construction. In G. Kenyon, E. Bohlmeijer, & W. Randall (Eds.), *Storying later life: Issues, investigations, and interventions in narrative gerontology* (pp. 51-65). New York: Oxford University Press.

Langer, L. (1991). *Holocaust testimonies: The ruins of memory.* New Haven, CT: Yale University Press.

Lasair, S. (2019). A narrative approach to spirituality and spiritual care in health care. *Journal of Religion and Health, 59.* 1524-1540.

Laszlo, E. (2007). *Science and the Akashic field: An integral theory of everything* (2nd edition). Rochester, VT: Inner Tradition.

Le Guin, U. (1989). *Dancing at the edge of the world: Thoughts on words, women, places.* New York: Harper & Row.

Linde, C. (1993). *Life stories: The quest for coherence.* New York: Oxford University Press.

Long, J., & Perry, P. (2016). *God and the afterlife.* New York: HarperOne.

Magai, C., & McFadden, S. (Eds.) (1996). *Handbook of emotion, adult development, and aging.* San Diego, CA: Academic Press.

Marcia, J., & Josselson, R. (2013). Eriksonian personality research and its implications for psychotherapy. *Journal of Personality, 81*(6). 617-629.

Markus, H., & Nurius, P. (1986). Possible selves. *American Psychologist, 41*(9). 954-969.

May, R. (1991). The cry for myth. New York: W. W. Norton.

McAdams, D. (1996). Narrating the self in adulthood. In J. Birren, G. Kenyon, J-E. Ruth, J. Schroots & T. Svensson (Eds.), *Aging and biography: Explorations in adult development* (pp. 131-148). New York: Springer.

McAdams, D. (2001). *The person: An integrated introduction to personality psychology* (3rd ed.). New York: Harcourt.

McAdams, D. (2006). *The redemptive self: Stories Americans live by.* New York: Oxford University Press.

McAdams, D. (2008). Personal narratives and the life story. In O. John, R. Robins, & L. Pervin (Eds.), *Handbook of personality: Theory and research* (3rd edition). (pp. 242-262). New York: Guilford.

McCullough, L. (1993). Arrested aging: The power of the past to make us aged and old. In T. Cole, W. Achenbaum, P. Jakobi, & R. Kastenbaum (Eds.), *Voices and visions of aging: Toward a critical gerontology* (pp. 184-204). New York: Springer.

McFadden, S., & Atchley, R. (Eds.) (2001). *Aging and the meaning of time: A multidisciplinary exploration.* New York: Springer.

McKendy, J. (2006). "I'm very careful about that": Narrative agency of men in prison. *Discourse & Society, 17*(4). 473-502.

McLeod, J. (1997). *Narrative and psychotherapy.* London: Sage.

McTaggart, L. (2002). *The field: The quest for the secret force of the universe.* New York: HarperCollins.

de Medeiros, K. (2011). Telling stories: How do expressions of self differ in a writing group versus a reminiscence group? In G. Kenyon, E. Bohlmeijer, & W. Randall (Eds.), *Storying later life: Issues, investigations, and interventions in narrative gerontology* (pp. 159-176). New York: Oxford University Press.

de Medeiros, K., & Rubinstein, R. (2015). "Shadow stories" in oral interviews: Narrative care through careful listening. *Journal of Aging Studies, 34.* 162-168.

Miller, J. (1978). The problematic of ending in narrative. *Nineteenth-Century Fiction 33*(1), 3-7.
Missine, L. (2003). The search for meaning in life in older age. In A. Jewel (Ed.), *Ageing, spirituality, and well-being* (pp. 113-123). London: Jessica Kingsley.
Moody, H. (1995). Mysticism. In M. Kimble, S. McFadden, J. Ellor, & J. Seeber (Eds.), *Aging, spirituality, and religion: A handbook* (pp. 87-101). Minneapolis, MN: Augsburg Fortress
Moore, T. (1992). *Care of the soul: A guide for cultivating depth and sacredness in everyday life.* New York: HarperCollins.
Moore, T. (2017). *The ageless soul.* New York: St. Martin's.
Morson, G. (1994). *Narrative and freedom: The shadows of time.* New Haven, CT: Yale University Press.
Myerhoff, B. (1992). *Remembered lives: The work of ritual, storytelling, and growing older.* Ann Arbor, MI: The University of Michigan Press.
Myss, C. (1996). *Anatomy of the spirit: The seven stages of power and healing.* New York: Three Rivers Press.
Napier, N. (1993). Living our stories: Discovering and replacing limiting family myths. In C. Simpkinson & A. Simpkinson (Eds.), *Sacred stories: A celebration of the power of stories to transform and heal.* (pp. 143-156). San Francisco: HarperCollins.
Neisser, U., & Libby, L. (2000). Remembering life experiences. In E. Tulving & F. Craik (Eds.), *The Oxford handbook of memory.* (pp. 315-332). New York: Oxford University Press.
Nelson, H. (2001). *Damaged identities: Narrative repair.* Ithaca, NY: Cornell University Press.
Nola, L. (2007). *Listography: Your life in lists.* San Francisco, CA: Chronicle Books.
Noonan, D. (2011). The ripple effect: A story of the transformational nature of narrative care. In G. Kenyon, E. Bohlmeijer, & W. Randall (Eds.), *Storying later life: Issues, investigations, and interventions in narrative gerontology* (pp. 354-365). New York: Oxford University Press.
Nouwen, H. (1976). *Reaching out: The three movements of the spiritual life.* London: Collins.
Nouwen, H., & Gaffney, W. (1976). *Aging: The fulfillment of life.* Garden City, NY: Anchor.
Osis, M., & Stout, L. (2001). Using narrative therapy with older clients. In G. Kenyon, P. Clark, & B. de Vries (Eds.), *Narrative gerontology: Theory, research, and practice* (pp. 273-290). New York: Springer.

Palmer, P. (2018). *On the brink of everything: Grace, gravity, and getting old*. New York: Berrett-Koehler.

Pennebaker, J., & Seagal, J. (1999). Forming a story: The health benefits of narrative. *Journal of Clinical Psychology, 55*(10). 1243-1254.

Phillips, J. (1954). *Your God is too small*. London: SCM.

Pickover, C. (2015). *The physics devotional: Celebrating the wisdom and beauty of physics*. New York: Sterling.

Pipher, M. (1999). *Another country: Navigating the emotional terrain of our elders*. New York: Riverhead.

Plato. (1953). *The Republic*. (D. Lee, Trans.). London: Penguin. (Original work composed 360 BCE).

Pohlman, B. (2003). Storytelling circles: Stories of age and aging. *Generations, 27*(3). 44-48.

Polkinghorne, D. (1988). *Narrative knowing and the human sciences*. Albany, NY: State University of New York Press.

Price, J. (2008). *The woman who can't forget: A memoir*. New York: Free Press.

Prickett, S. (2002). *Narrative, religion and science: Fundamentalism versus irony*. Cambridge, UK: Cambridge University Press.

Progoff, I. (1975). *At a journal workshop: The basic text and guide for using the intensive journal*. New York: Dialogue House Library.

Rainer, T. (1998). *Your life as story: Discovering the "new autobiography" and writing memoir as literature*. New York: Jeremy Tarcher.

Ramsey, J., & Blieszner, R. (2013). *Spiritual resiliency and aging: Hope, relationality, and the creative self*. Amityville, NY: Baywood.

Randall, C. (in preparation). *Coming full circle: Diaries of a polio survivor*.

Randall, W. (2015). *The narrative complexity of ordinary life: Tales from the coffee shop*. New York: Oxford University Press.

Randall, W. (2014). Lives as sacred texts: Toward a narrative theology of aging. *Caring Connections: An Inter-Lutheran Journal for Practitioners and Teachers of Pastoral Care and Counselling. 11*(4). 1-7.

Randall, W. (2014/1995). *The stories we are: An essay on self-creation* (2nd edition). Toronto, ON: University of Toronto Press.

Randall, W. (2013). The importance of being ironic: Narrative openness and personal resilience in later life. *The Gerontologist. 53*(1). 9-16.

Randall, W. (2010a). Storywork: Autobiographical learning in later life. In C. Clark & M. Rossiter (Eds.), *Narrative perspectives on adult education: New directions for adult and continuing education, 126*. (pp. 25-36). San Francisco, CA: Jossey-Bass.

Randall, W. (2010b). The narrative complexity of our past: In praise of memory's sins. *Theory & Psychology, 20*(2). 1-23.

Randall, W. (2009). Transcending our stories: A narrative perspective on spirituality in later life. *Critical Social Work, 10*(1).

Randall, W. (1999). Narrative intelligence and the novelty of our lives. *Journal of Aging Studies, 13*(1), 11-28.

Randall, W. Sr. (2000). *Showers of blessing: Memoir of a preacher, teacher, and singer.* Fredericton, NB.

Randall, W. Sr. (2004). *Guidelines to my ancestors: Randalls, Rings, Roberts, Grays.* Fredericton, NB.

Randall, W., Achenbaum, A., & Lewis, B. (in preparation). *New meanings from old tales: Stories for the second half of life.*

Randall, W., Baldwin, C, McKenzie-Mohr, S., McKim, E., & Furlong, D. (2015). Narrative and resilience: A comparative analysis of how older adults story their lives. *Journal of Aging Studies, 34.* 155-161

Randall, W., & Kenyon, G. (2002). Reminiscence as reading our lives: Toward a wisdom environment. In J. Webster & B. Haight (Eds.), *Critical advances in reminiscence: Theoretical, empirical, and clinical perspectives* (pp. 233-253). New York: Springer.

Randall, W., & Kenyon, G. (2001). *Ordinary wisdom: Biographical aging and the journey of life.* Westport, CT: Praeger.

Randall, W., & Khurshid, K. (2017). Narrative development in later life: A novel perspective. *Age, Culture, Humanities: An Interdisciplinary Journal, 3.*

Randall, W., & McKim, E. (2008). *Reading our lives: The poetics of growing old.* New York: Oxford University Press.

Randall, W., Prior, S., & Skarborn, M. (2006). How listeners shape what tellers tell: Patterns of interaction in lifestory interviews and their impact on reminiscence with elderly interviewees. *Journal of Aging Studies, 20.* 381-396.

Randall, W., & Robinson, M. (in preparation). *Things that matter: Resilience, reminiscence, and the role of special objects in the stories of our lives.* Toronto, ON: University of Toronto Press.

Ray, R. (2000). *Beyond Nostalgia: Aging and life-story writing.* Charlottesville,VA: Unversity Press of Virginia.

Rosen, H. (1986). The importance of story. *Language Arts. 63*(3). 226-237.

Ruffing, J. (2011). *To tell the sacred tale: Spiritual direction and narrative.* Mahwah, NJ: Paulist.

Ruffing, J. (2003). To tell the sacred tale: Spiritual direction and narrative. *New Theology Review, 16*(3). 38-52.

Rushdie, S. (1992). One thousand days in a balloon. In *Imaginary homelands: Essays and criticism 1981-1991* (pp. 430-439). London: Penguin.

Ruth, J-E., & Kenyon, G. (1996). Biography in adult development and aging. In J. Birren, G. Kenyon, J-E. Ruth, J. Schroots, & T. Svensson (Eds.), *Aging and biography: Explorations in adult development* (pp. 1-20). New York: Springer.

Rybarczyk, B., & Bellg, A. (1997). *Listening to life stories: A new approach to stress intervention in health care*. New York: Springer.

Sacks, O. (1987). *The man who mistook his wife for a hat and other clinical tales*. New York: Harper Collins.

Sagan, C. (1985). *Contact: A novel*. New York: Simon and Schuster.

Sanders, E. (2007). *The LifeBio Memory Journal*. Marysville, OH: LifeBio Inc.

Sarbin, T. (1986). The narrative as a root metaphor for psychology. In T. Sarbin (Ed.), *Narrative psychology: The storied nature of human conduct* (pp. 3-21). New York: Praeger.

Sarton, M. (1977). *Journal of a solitude*. New York: W. W. Norton.

Sarton, M. (1981). *The house by the sea*. New York: W. W. Norton.

Sarton, M. (1980). *Recovering: A journal*. New York: W. W. Norton.

Scheib, K. (2016). *Pastoral care: Telling the stories of our lives*. Nashville, TN: Abingdon.

Scheib, K. (2019). *Attend to stories: How to flourish in ministry*. United Methodist Church.

Scott-Maxwell, F. (1968). *The measure of my days*. London: Penguin.

Schachter-Shalomi, Z. & Miller, R. (1995). *From age-ing to sage-ing: A profound new vision of growing older*. New York: Warner.

Schank, R. (1990). *Tell me a story: A new look at real and artificial intelligence*. New York: Scribner's.

Sherman, E. (1991). Reminiscentia: Cherished objects as memorabilia in late-life reminiscence. *International Journal of Aging and Human Development. 33*(2). 89-100.

Singer, J., & Skerrett, K. (2014). *Positive couple therapy: Using we-stories to enhance resilience*. New York: Routledge.

Skerrett, K. (2018). *Tell me again how I know you? An adoptee's quest for belonging*. Winnipeg, MB: ArtBookbindery.

Spector-Mersel, G. (2017). Life story reflection in social work education: A practical model. *Journal of Social Work Education, 53*(2). 286-299.

Spence, D. (1982). *Narrative truth and historical truth*. New York: W.W. Norton.

Staude, J. (2005). Autobiography as a spiritual practice. *Journal of Gerontological Social Work, 45*(3). 249-269.

Stone, E. (2004). *Black sheep and kissing cousins: How our family stories shape us.* Piscataway, NJ: Transaction Publishers.

Stone, R. (1996). *The healing power of storytelling: A sacred journey of personal discovery.* New York: Hyperion.

Stroup, G. (1981). *The promise of narrative theology.* Atlanta, GA: John Knox Press.

Swimme, B., & Berry, T. (1992). *The universe story: From the primordial flaring forth to the ecozoic era - a celebration of the unfolding of the cosmos.* San Francisco, CA: HarperSanFrancisco.

Synnes, O. (2015). Narratives of nostalgia in the face of death: The importance of lighter stories of the past in palliative care. *Journal of Aging Studies, 34.* 169-176.

Taha, I. (1998-99). Openness and closedness: Four categories of closurization in modern Arabic fiction. *Journal of Arabic and Islamic Studies 2,* 1-23.

TeSelle, S. (1975a). *Speaking in parables: A study in metaphor and theology.* Philadelphia, PA: Fortress Press.

TeSelle, S. (1975b). The experience of coming to belief. *Theology Today, 32*(2). 159-165.

Tolle, E. (2003). *Stillness speaks.* Vancouver, BC: Namaste.

Tornstam, L. (1996). Gerotranscendence: A theory about maturing into old age. *Journal of Aging and Identity 1*(1), 37-49.

Truitt, A. (1987). *Turn: The journal of an artist.* London: Penguin.

Turner, M. (1996). *The literary mind.* New York: Oxford University Press.

Vaillant, G. (2015). *Triumphs of experience: The men of the Harvard Grant Study.* Cambridge, MA: Harvard University Press.

Van Diepen, M. (2014). *True Doors.* www.truedoors.com

Villar, F., & Serrat, R. (2017). Changing the culture of long-term care through narrative care: Individual, interpersonal, and institutional dimensions. *Journal of Aging Studies, 40.* 44-48.

Vonnegut, K. (1982). *Deadeye Dick.* New York: Dell.

Wakefield, D. (1990). *The story of your life: Writing a spiritual autobiography.* Boston, MA: Beacon.

Wall, S. & Arden, H. (2006). *Wisdomkeepers: Meetings with Native American spiritual elders.* Hillsboro, OR: Beyond Words.

Wang, Q. (2013). *The autobiographical self in time and culture.* New York: Oxford University Press.

Waxman, B. (1997). *To live in the center of the moment: Literary autobiographies of aging.* Charlottesville, VA: University of Virginia Press.

Westwood, M., Keats, P., & Wilensky, P. (2003). Therapeutic enactment: Integrating individual and group counselling models for change. *The Journal for Specialists in Social Work, 28*(2). 122-138.

White, M., & Epston, D. (1990). *Narrative means to therapeutic ends.* New York: W. W. Norton.

Wilson, E. O. (September, 2014). On free will and how the brain is like a colony of ants. *Harper's Magazine*, 49-52.

Wingard, B., & Lester, J. (2001). *Telling our stories in ways that make us stronger.* Adelaide, AU: Dulwich Centre Publications.

Wink, P., & Schiff, B. (2002). To review or not to review? The role of personality and life events in life review and adaptation to older age. In J. Webster & B. Haight (Eds.), *Critical advances in reminiscence: From theory to application* (pp. 44-60). New York: Springer.

Winquist, C. (1980). *Practical hermeneutics: A revised agenda for the ministry.* Chico, CA: Scholars Press.

Wong, P.T. (1995). The processes of adaptive reminiscence. In B. Haight & J. Webster (Eds.), *The art and science of reminiscing: Theory, research, methods and applications* (pp. 23-35). Washington, DC: Taylor & Francis.

Index

aging as adventure, 79, 100, 140
aging as discovery, 29
aging as natural monastery, 33f
ambiguity, 25
Alchemist, The, 46
Alcoholics Anonymous, 76
Angelou, Maya, 112, 120
arrested aging, 111
Atkinson, Robert, 141
Atwood, Margaret, 92
Auschwitz, 95f
autobiographical development, 68
autobiographical drive, 61
autobiographical learning, 47
autobiographical memory, 51f
autobiographical reasoning, 76
autobiographical self, 109

Baldwin, Christina, 141
Baldwin, Clive, 86, 90, 137
Bateson, Mary Catherine, 49, 55
Bellg, Albert, 113
Berman, Harry, 78
Berry, Thomas, 38, 89
Beuchner, Frederick, 47
Bible, The, 41
big story narrative reflection, 75, 139
biographical aging, 7, 48
biography and biology, 58
Birren, Jim, 133
Bohlmeijer, Ernst, 98
Boisen, Anton, 14, 65
brain fitness, 20
Bridges, William, 56, 95
Brundage, Don, 144
Bruner, Jerome, 50f, 59, 68, 105
burnout, 113
Butala, Sharon, 96

CDRS, 83
Celebrating Our Stories, 132f

Charon, Rita, 114
cherished objects, 129
China, 109
Chopra, Deepak, 29f
Christianity, 25, 33, 41f
CIRN, 83
closed closure, 162
closure, 139, 161f
co-authoring, 108
Coelho, Paul, 46
Cohen, Gene, 23, 61, 79
coherence, 91, 149
Coleman, Peter, 77
Coles, Robert, 126, 164
Contact, 30f, 46
contaminated sequence, 89f
conversation, 134f
conversion, 42f
cosmic story, 44
counterfactuals, 54
counter-stories, 131
creative reminiscence, 132
crisis of meaning, 60
Crisp, Jane, 137
culture, 109f

Dante, Alighieri, 88
death, 28f, 138-140
decline, 20
deep old age, 100, 163
de Lange, Frits, 100
de Medeiros, Kate, 133, 149
dementia, 136-138
de-storying, 91, 110
developmental tasks, 74
dialogical self, 54f
differentiation, 72, 84
disengagement, 33

ego integrity, 74
elder, 10, 79, 99, 163

emotional regulation, 23
encore phase, 79
epilogue time, 97
Epston, David, 96
Erikson, Erik, 22, 28, 53, 74f
escapist reminscence, 77

faces without stories, 111
faction, 52
failed story, 90
fairy tales, 147
faith, 29f, 44
family stories, 106f, 130
feeling tone, 127
Ford, Henry, 11
Fowler, James, 29f
Frank, Arthur, 105, 124
Freeman, Mark, 47, 75, 91, 97
Friedan, Betty, 79, 99f
Frye, Northrop, 41
Fulford, Robert, 86
full circle, 12, 32
fundamentalism, 42

gender, 55
genealogy, 27
generative narration, 79
generative transference, 79
generativity, 28, 75
gerontology, 7, 14, 19, 34
gerotranscendence, 27
God, 30f
good life story, 72, 82
good strong story, 11, 59, 82
Greene, Graham, 55
growing old vs getting old, 20, 47, 99
Guest, Edgar A., 124
guided autobiography, 133, 149

Haley, Alex, 54
Hamkins, SuEllen, 131
Hammerskjöld, Dag, 26
Hampl, Patricia, 47, 150
Harvard University, 37
Hauerwas, Stanley, 143
Haught, John, 43f

Hayflick, Leonard, 158
Hedelund, Morten, 134
hermeneutical gerontology, 78
Hillman, James, 7
historical truth, 138
Holmes, Oliver Wendell, 70f
horizon of self-understanding, 78
Hydén, Lars-Christer, 138
hyperthymestic syndrome, 52

identity, 53-59
identity as a lifestory, 53
identity crisis, 53, 60
identity foreclosure, 72
illusions, 24
immune system, 135
inside vs outside of aging, 19f
instrumental reminiscence, 77
integrative reminiscence, 77
interpretive openness, 100
iron lung story, 54, 71, 150-154
ironic orientation, 24, 38, 154
Islam, 33

Josselson, Ruthellen, 109
Jourard, Sidney, 106
journalling, 148
journey inward, 26
Jung, Carl, 161f

Kazin, Alfred, 36
Keen, Sam, 92
Kellerman, Jonathan, 88
Kennedy, Eugene, 127
Kenyon, Gary, 5, 14, 47, 88, 127
King, Thomas, 94f
Kleinman, Arthur, 112
Kottler, Jeffrey, 126, 150
Kuhl, David, 141

landscape of action, 59, 73
landscape of consciousness, 59, 73
LaFleur, Richard, 134
Langer, Lawrence, 95
Lazlo, Ervin, 39
legacy, 80

LeGuin, Ursula, 91
Lester, Jane, 120
library of our lives, 54
life harvesting, 79
life review, 22f, 75, 139
life scripts, 107
Linde, Charlotte, 69
Lindemann, Hilde, 138
listening disability, 121
listening styles, 121
lists, 132, 146
literary mind, 45, 50
lives as parables, 44-47
logical thought, 51, 111
long view, 22, 31

Maritime Provinces, 108
master narrative, 36ff
McAdams, Dan, 53f, 71-74, 78, 89
McCullough, Lawrence, 111
McKendy, John, 91
McKim, Elizabeth, 15, 81
McLeod, John, 125
McTaggart, Lynne, 39
meaning, 50, 60, 70
melancholy, 23
memories as anomalies, 52
meta-narrative, 36
metaphor, 25, 45
metaphysical agoraphobia, 89
Miller, J. Hillis, 140
Moody, Rick, 33
Moore, Thomas, 20f, 107
moral injury, 93, 113
Music and Memory, 138
multiple fluid narratives, 49
Myerhoff, Barbara, 76
Myss, Carolyn, 58
mythic stage, 72-73

Napier, Nancy, 106
narrative agency, 130
narrative anemia, 112
narrative arrest, 111
narrative atrophy, 87, 111
narrative care, 9, 81, 85, 115, 119-155

narrative challenges, 85-99
narrative coherence, 91, 137
narrative compaction, 112
narrative constipation, 112
narrative contamination, 89
narrative debris, 91f
narrative deprivation, 86
narrative development, 65-81
narrative diarrhea, 112
narrative disengagement, 140
narrative diminution, 98
narrative disjuncture, 95
narrative disorientation, 88
narrative dispossession, 90
narrative disruption, 92
narrative dissonance, 95
narrative domination, 94
narrative entanglement, 138
narrative environment, 104-110
narrative ethics, 137
narrative foreclosure, 72, 97f, 123
narrative gerontology, 14, 48-50
narrative identity, 53-59, 100
narrative imagination, 147
narrative imprisonment, 94f
narrative incoherence, 91
narrative indigestion, 112
narrative intelligence, 51
narrative knots, 87f
narrative literacy, 145
narrative loneliness, 134
narrative loss, 86
narrative lostness, 88
narrative medicine, 110-115
narrative of decline, 20
narrative openness, 95, 99f, 157-164
narrative paradigm, 9
narrative phase, 60-62
narrative pregnancy, 112
narrative psychiatry, 131
narrative psychology, 50f
narrative quilting, 137
narrative reflection, 75
narrative repair, 115
narrative resilience, 83-85
narrative resources, 38

narrative root metaphor, 53
narrative self-care, 143-145
narrative septicemia, 112
narrative tasks, 8, 61, 74-81
narrative templates, 38, 107
narrative theology, 13, 39-44
narrative therapy, 96, 125, 133f
narrative thought, 50f, 60, 113
narrative tone, 56, 127
narrative truth, 138, 141
narrative unconscious, 37
narrative unsustainability, 90
narrative variable, 16
narrative vs story, 16
National Hockey League, 12
near death experiences, 139
negative life events, 60
Nikolasjen, Andreas, 134
Nola, Lisa, 132
Norway, 108
nostalgic stories, 139, 158
novelty of our lives, 65
nuclear episodes, 130

obsessive reminiscence, 77
Old Testament, The, 40f
open closure, 162
openness, 99f
open stories, open lives, 101
outside of aging, 19
ordinary wisdom, 135

Palmer, Parker, 24
parable, 44f
parabolic potential, 46, 100
paradigmatic thought, 51
patient-centered care, 114
personal myth, 53
Phillips, J. B., 30
philosophic homework, 20, 98, 163
philosophical deepening, 148
philosophical openness, 45
Pipher, Mary, 83
poetics, 15
polio, 11f, 150f
Polkinghorne, Donald, 68f

positivity effect, 24
possible selves, 77
post-formal thought, 25
post-mythic stage, 73f, 78, 100
preferred narratives, 130
pre-mythic stage, 71f
preservative care, 138
problem-saturated stories, 125
Progoff, Ira, 148
psychotherapy, 125
PTSD, 93

Rainer, Tristine, 148
Randall, Carol, 11f, 150-153
Randall, Donna, 10f, 66, 80, 153
Randall, William Sr, 10f, 79, 157-161
Ray, Ruth, 49f
reading our lives, 15, 81
re-assembling, 76
reconciliation, 77f
recontextualizing, 78
recycling, 79
redemptive sequence, 89
re-genre-ation, 78, 136
re-membering, 76
reminiscence, 77, 129, 132
reminiscence bump, 80
reminiscence types, 77
resilience, 83-85
re-storying, 69, 73
revising the plot, 68f, 73, 110
Ruffing, Janet, 59, 142
ruminescence, 80
Rushdie, Salman, 94
Rybarczyk, Bruce, 113

Sacks, Oliver, 114
sacred masterplots, 36, 88
sacred stories, 142
sacred tales, 131
sacred text, 46
Sagan, Carl, 30f
Sarbin, Theodore, 53
Sarton, May, 69f, 86, 112, 141
Schacter-Shalomi, Zalman, 79, 163
Scheib, Karen, 36, 119, 142

Schwartz, Joseph, 39
science, 31, 37, 39
Scott-Maxwell, Florida, 28f, 81, 140
self as story, 143
SETI, 30
shadow CV, 154f
shadow stories, 58, 130
signature stories, 54, 130, 153
Skerrett, Karen, 148f
slow questions, 34
social emotional selectivity, 24
socio-narratology, 105
soul, 21
soul injury, 93
Spector-Mersel, Gabriela, 75
spiritual aging, 21, 48
spiritual development, 71
spiritual eldering, 79, 99
spirituality and narrative, 35, 47
spirituality vs religion, 35
St. Augustine, 48
St. Thomas University, 14
Stone, Elizabeth, 106
Stone, Richard, 51
story catchers, 138, 141
story companions, 142, 164
storykeepers, 138, 159
storylistening, 120-136, 167-170
story logic, 51
story-talk, 53
storytelling circles, 133
story vs narrative, 16
storywork, 146
storyworld, 56, 65-71, 131-135
storying style, 56f, 121, 129f
storyotyping, 90
survivor guilt, 12, 153
Swimme, Brian, 39
Synnes, Oddgeir, 139, 159

Tennyson, Alfred Lord, 108
The Chambered Nautilius, 71
therapeutic enactment, 93
therapy, 125-127
time, 27
TimeSlips, 138

time-stretching, 148
Tolle, Echkart, 90
Tornstam, Lars, 27f
transmissive reminiscence, 77
trouble, 34, 60
True Doors, 138
Truitt, Anne, 69
truth, 29, 37, 141

universe story, 39
unlived lives, 77
untold stories, 58

Veterans Transition Project, 93
vicious cycle, 90
Vonnegut, Kurt, 97

Wakefield, Dan, 148
Wang, Qi, 109
we-stories, 58
Westerhof, Gerben, 98
Westwood, Marvin, 93, 134
White, Michael, 96
Williams, William Carlos, 126, 164
Wilson, Edmund O., 50
Wingard, Barbara, 120
Winquist, Charles, 127
wisdom, 49f, 135, 163f
wisdom environment, 49, 101, 148
wisdomkeepers, 159
wonder, 29

www.ingramcontent.com/pod-product-compliance
Lightning Source LLC
Chambersburg PA
CBHW020930090426
42736CB00010B/1093